ALL THE PREACHER'S WIVES

A Peek Behind The Curtain Of Being A Preacher's Wife

If you purchased this book without a cover, you should be aware that this book is stolen property. It was reported as "unsold and destroyed" to the publisher, and neither the author nor the publisher has received any payments for this "stripped book."

ALL THE PREACHER'S WIVES, AN ANTHOLOGY
A Peek Behind The Curtain Of Being A Preacher's Wife

THE HOLY BIBLE, NEW INTERNATIONAL VERSION®, NIV®
Copyright © 1973, 1978, 1984, 2011 by Biblica, Inc. ® Used by permission.
All rights reserved worldwide.

Texts credited to Clear Word are from *The Clear Word*, copyright © 1994, 2000, 2003, 2004 by Review and Herald Publishing Association. All rights reserved.

The body of work titled All The Preacher's Wives, An Anthology, Copyright © 2022 by N.D. "Indy" Brennan

Cover Design by MADDCity MEDIA

Website: https://www.allthepreacherswives.com

No part of this publication may be reproduced, stored in a retrieval system, or transmitted in any form or by any means, electronic, mechanical, photocopying, recording, or otherwise, without the written permission of the publisher. the only exception is brief quotations in printed reviews. For information regarding permission, contact N. D. "Indy" Brennan at ndbrennanauthor@gmail.com or on Instagram @ndbrennanauthor.

This book was originally published by arrangement with MADDCity MEDIA, The Jade Chrysalis LLC, and Pa-Pro-Vi Publishing, Inc.

Dr. Velma Bagby, Chosen Bolton, Carolyn Coleman, Josie Cooper, TreSonya Madison Durden, MaLena Evans, Gina Fields, Undrea Gray, Jaime Haddock, Dorothy Henley, Krystal Henry, Latesha Higgs, Liza Hines, Patricia Jackson, Melanie M. Johnson, Merl Johnson, Linda Kornegay, Brandie Manigault, Dr. Nina McGhee, Trivia Payne, and Tenelle Torrence, Authors

ALL THE PREACHER'S WIVES / An Anthology - First Edition

1. Relationship 2. Marriage 3. Relationship
4. Christian 5. Marriage 6. Couples I. N. D. "Indy" Brennan, Author II. All The Preacher's Wives, Title

ISBN - 978-1-959667-11-7

This book was arranged by N. D. "Indy" Brennan of MADDCity Media.

All rights reserved.

Typeset Garamond

ALL THE PREACHER'S WIVES
A Peek Behind The Curtain Of Being A Preacher's Wife

DEDICATION

This anthology is dedicated to women who have felt the need to bridle their tongues for the sake of the ministry or humility. Through this book, you are encouraged to speak with God-given authority. We want you to realize that you are God's greatest greatness. So, dare to be intentional. Through Christ, there is nothing you can't do.

Additionally, this book is dedicated to the men who have the courage to love us with their whole heart. Thank you for your continued love and support.

May God bless every hand that touches or reads this book.

ALL THE PREACHER'S WIVES
A Peek Behind The Curtain Of Being A Preacher's Wife

ALL THE PREACHER'S WIVES
A Peek Behind The Curtain Of Being A Preacher's Wife

TABLE OF CONTENTS

	Foreword by Latesha Higgs	v
1	**God's In Love With A Stripper** by Pastor Dorothy Henley	1
2	**You Are Stronger Than You Think** by Liza Hines	17
3	**Praise God Anyhow** by Dr. Velma Bagby	29
4	**Relationship With The Master** by Author Melanie "The Voice" Johnson	43
5	**The Fear In Love** by Pastor Brandie Manigault	55
6	**To Be Or Not To Be A Preacher's Wife** by Dr. Trivia Payne	69
7	**Can You Handle My Truth** by Pastor Patricia Jackson	83
8	**Vibrations Of Broken Silence** by Coach Krystal Henry	95
9	**Understanding The Marriage Assignment** by Tenelle Torrence	109
10	**One Plus One Equals One** by TreSonya Madison Durden	127
11	**The Unforeseen Gift: Being A Pastor's Wife** by Author Linda P. Kornegay	141
12	**Just As I Am** by MaLena Evans	153
13	**Molding Clay** by Merl Johnson	163
14	**Lost While Under The Influence** by Apostle Chosen Boston	177
15	**Products Of Our Environment** by Pastor Josie Cooper	195
16	**For The Love Of God** by Petra (Anonymous)	205
17	**Hindsight Is 20/20** by Dr. Nina McGhee	217

TABLE OF CONTENTS

18	**From Broken To Blessed**	227
	by Undrea "Shay" Gray	
19	**From Sundays To The Sabbath Day**	241
	by Gina Fields	
20	**The Dating Game**	263
	by Pastor Jamie Haddock	
	About The Author	275

FOREWORD BY LATESHA HIGGS

The eldest granddaughter of Reverend Dr. Nathaniel Higgs Sr., community activist and former pastor of Southern Baptist Church in Baltimore, Maryland

Though I'm not the wife of a preacher, I have witnessed the seriousness of its calling through my grandmother. Her husband, my beloved grandfather, was not only a Baptist pastor but a community activist. He was a man of noble character and did many wonderful things in the communities that God called him to serve. My grandfather, whom I affectionately called "Granddaddy," was both my hero and role model. As great as my grandfather was, let's not forget that next to every strong man stands an equally strong and powerful woman. My grandmother, Bernice Higgs, was that woman. She was his ordained helpmate who lovingly served, honored, and supported him until his last days. Granny, as I lovingly called her, was a very active First Lady. She sang in the choir (engaging people in the worship experience with her soulful voice), aided in the Christian Education Ministry (Vacation Bible School, Bible Discovery Hour, etc.), and assisted with some of the administrative tasks of the church. You name it and Granny was part of it. I have fond memories of helping her with the church's bulletin board displays and other minor tasks. She was a humble and quiet woman yet could fill any room with a bold and powerful presence. As the proverbial saying goes, she was one to "speak softly and carry a big stick!"

While in high school, I was blessed to see the call over my grandparents' lives. For two years, I lived with them and received valuable insight into the life of a preacher's wife. It was then that I learned that the life of a preacher's wife is not all glory and glamor as some falsely believe. What many fail to realize is that when God calls the man to shepherd his people, he's also calling his wife into a life of ministry. It is a life that comes with all manner of spiritual warfare. The

ALL THE PREACHER'S WIVES
A Peek Behind The Curtain Of Being A Preacher's Wife

woman assigned to this ministry, for it is a ministry, must be clothed in the full armor of God, embrace wisdom, and possess a keen, discerning spirit. Above all, the woman assigned to this ministry must be able to operate in the fullness of God's love (1 Corinthians 13:4-8). As her husband's ordained helpmate, the wife of a preacher prays for and over him, serves God's people alongside him, and is emblematic of a Proverbs 31 woman to other women in the ministry. The wife of a preacher is more than just a role. It is an assignment from God. I like to think that just as Aaron and Hur were to Moses when Joshua and the Israelites totally defeated the Amalekites, so too are the wives of preachers.

Whether or not you are the wife of a preacher, this book is a great read as it sheds light on the power and strength necessary to withstand the attacks of the enemy—something all women can benefit from. Upon careful reading of the stories, you will gain strategies and tools on how to operate in your God-given assignment. In this book, you will read about the many challenges, trials, and obstacles the wives of preachers face while operating within their God-given assignment. These are more than just lived experiences. The stories you are about to read are stories of resilience, grace, and triumph. The women who have shared these stories are women who have a love for God and His people. Their stories also remind us of the true power and strength of women—God's chosen helpmate for man. As you take a peek into their lives, may you be inspired to earnestly lift up in prayer, not only your pastor and his loving wife but all women in the ministry.

Dorothy Henley

"While she was in church, waving her hands, crying, and singing praises to the pillars; I was at home kicking and fighting, being cornered, choked, and forced to scream into my pillow."

ALL THE PREACHER'S WIVES
A Peek Behind The Curtain Of Being A Preacher's Wife

1
GOD'S IN LOVE WITH A STRIPPER

Having been licensed in ministry since 1999, I've seen my fair share of what goes on behind the scenes in "church" as it relates to the treatment of women pastors and Pastors' wives. Firstly, over the years I have served as more than merely a member of the church. I have served as Evangelist, Associate Minister, Assistant to the pastor, and Youth Leader-Pastor as I evolved spiritually. Busy doesn't begin to describe the time and effort I've put into ministry. Even today, I am the Evangelist-Pastor of God's Peace & Blessings Church, Inc. - A Church Without Walls. Our focus is on street ministry and mobile evangelism. In fact, the church's motto is: "We Always Keep it 100 Because 99 and a half Just Won't Do." Contrary to R&B Artist Jamie Foxx, you won't be able to "Blame It on the Alcohol" after reading this. We proudly "Keep it 100" while giving it to you "straight with no chaser!"

THE FATHERS:

My Father, Ike, died when I was 15 years old. He was nearly sixty years when I was born. My father told me that he never went past the first grade in school because he had to quit school to work in the cotton and tobacco fields to take care of his sibling after their mother - my paternal grandmother - suddenly died. He never learned to really

ALL THE PREACHER'S WIVES
A Peek Behind The Curtain Of Being A Preacher's Wife

read or write but he could most certainly count. He said he learned to count because he needed to make certain his wages from picking cotton and tobacco were correct. He signed his name with an "X" until my mother, Ivory, who was 29 years his junior, taught him how to write his name and read the word "STOP" on the stop sign.

My mother was extremely active in the church and made certain her six children, my five siblings and me, were too. I was baptized at the age of 8 and my parents divorced when I was 10. Both of my parents remarried.

My father married my stepmom, a woman 39 years his junior. She was very active in the Holiness Church. My younger sister and I loved going to worship there whenever we spent weekends and summers with my dad. The pastor of the Holiness church was a single man with a congregation filled with young and middle-aged single women with children. The musicians were all male too. It was much different from our Baptist church. It was lit! The music was fast-paced and upbeat. The people sang loudly and clapped their hands hard and high. They would cry, run around the church, speak in tongues, and fall out on the floor and a white sheet would be placed over them. The male musicians played the pianos, drums, and guitars while the women and/or children in the congregation strummed the washboard with a metal spoon and beat the tambourines. The people would scream and shout until they had little to no voice by the end of the service. They would dance themselves into a trance until the music stopped and started up again. Sweat would be pouring from these women in the congregation like someone had doused them with a bucket of water. The more they sweated, the wetter and clingier their dresses became, which in turn encouraged the pastor to sing louder and the musicians to play longer.

Of course, there was the prayer line at the end of service which included anointing with oil and the laying on of hands by the pastor to heal infirmities affecting these women in their breast, abdomen, legs, hips, and thigh regions. Needless to say, this wolf in sheep's clothing went on to fornicate with single women in the church. He impregnated one of his married parishioners which led to her getting a divorce. She had two little girls at the time. He later married the parishioner he impregnated, and one child was born out of their union. The pastor, however, molested the two older girls, the half-sisters to the younger daughter. The pastor was shot and killed several years later by a family member of the two sisters he molested, his stepdaughters.

My mother, Ivory, remarried outside of her race after her divorce from my father. The pastor of the church at that time would not marry my mother and her Caucasian husband because he did not believe in interracial marriages. He preached weekly sermons on race-mixing being a sin. Interracial marriages in the red clay hills of Georgia were frowned upon and certainly not popular, especially in the 80s in the predominantly black middle-class neighborhood in which we lived and at the church where we worshipped.

Folk in the church began to talk and the pastor threatened to sit my mother down from singing in the choir and serving in the church. The pastor, his wife, and children had been to our home several times after church on Sunday. They would come over and have dinner with us frequently. He felt obliged to always get the first and biggest piece of chicken because he clearly loved my mom's cooking.

His wife, on the other hand, was a very nice lady who always pronounced my younger sister's name incorrectly but loved on us as if we were her own children. The pastor's wife, however, was not permitted to disagree with her husband or comment on anything he said or did, right or wrong, in public or in private dinner settings around parishioners. If she disagreed with him or expressed her opinion, she was quickly given a harsh rebuke by her husband, the pastor. According to him, her job was to serve him, keep the kids in line, and not ask too many questions. At the end of the worship service, she and the children had better beat him to the car rather than meet him at the

ALL THE PREACHER'S WIVES
A Peek Behind The Curtain Of Being A Preacher's Wife

car. Even if that meant she and the children had to wait an hour or more after service in the sweltering Georgia heat inside a car for him to come out of the church.

The older ladies in the kitchen would talk about him behind his back but smile in his face and change their tunes whenever he entered the room. They would simply shake their heads about the situation with his wife and the way he treated her. Unbeknownst to the pastor, because the food was to him what spinach is to Popeye the Sailor, (strength and courage) the older mothers working in the church kitchen would laugh amongst themselves about how badly they wanted to give the pastor's wife lessons on how to scold him with hot grits or grease for treating her the way he did. They, however, being older than both Pastor and his wife, never corrected him in love about the way he treated his wife.

I was somewhere between 8 and 10 years old when all these things took place. It wasn't until reflecting and writing this anthology that I realized these pastors' wives were at one time beautiful Vessels of Honor trying to build up the House of God only to end up being torn down by the so-called Man of God.

"Beware of false prophets, which come to you in sheep's clothing, but inwardly they are ravening wolves. [16] Ye shall know them by their fruit..." (Matthew 7:15-16, KJV)

In 1988, my mom met Ed, my stepfather. Again, mom was very active in the church and like in times of old, she made certain she took us to church every Sunday and any other day of the week that services were being held. Although we could opt out of going at 12 - the biblical age of consent according to my mother, not going to church was not an option especially living under her roof.

Ed transitioned in 2012 when I was 36 years old. I had just visited him in the hospital that Saturday, three days prior to his death.

ALL THE PREACHER'S WIVES
A Peek Behind The Curtain Of Being A Preacher's Wife

I gave him his last rights and communion in the hospital where we laughed, talked, joked, etc. Three days later, on a Tuesday at 9:00 PM, he would come home on Hospice. I was stationed at his bedside, reading scriptures to him as I choked back tears. I listened to his breathing become more labored. His heartbeat gradually grew fainter and fainter, and I watched his chest rise and fall for one final time as he took his last breath. My aunt, his sister, being a nurse, insisted that we bathe him before the coroners arrived. I had never bathed a corpse, but in August 2012 I had my first hands-on experience. I would later be asked by the family to eulogize my stepfather and preached for his Homegoing Service. The title of the sermon was "What have I gained from all of this?"

    I had been in ministry for 13 years when my stepfather died. As a minister in a congregation of nearly 300 people, I can't count on two hands without having fingers left over who in the congregation asked me if I was "Ok." Only the pastor and a couple of the Executive Ministry members attended the service. Sunday morning, just two days after his burial, it was business as usual at the church. Folk pulling you in every direction wanting your time and attention, prayers for their problems, and praise for their service in the church. Some might ask, "Well did they know you lost your stepfather?" Yes. The better question is: Did they really care? Some of the parishioners, mostly "seasoned saints" and so-called friends of our family, even had the nerve to tell me that they knew I hadn't slept in days and admonished me not to fall asleep during worship service.

    They said, "You're the worship leader and we need you to tone the bell, light the fire, and pump me up 'cuz the devil been busy this morning and I caught hell trying to get here this morning."

    I quickly responded with, "You do know I just buried my dad two days ago and I'm still grieving that loss?"

    Their counter was, "I thought he was your stepdad?"

    I replied, "You're correct, but he was like my dad because he was in my life for 24 of the 36 years I've been on this earth."

    These wonderful church folks followed up with, "Well, you're

ALL THE PREACHER'S WIVES
A Peek Behind The Curtain Of Being A Preacher's Wife

a preacher, so you'll be alright. Besides you of ALL people shouldn't be sad or crying over the loss of your stepfather. You know he's in a better place, heaven, with the Lord."

Honey, call me Fire Marshall Bill because I was HOT! I explained, "Lemme tell you something Sista! Despite what you might think, I'm HUMAN and last time I checked, Jesus not only SLEPT (Mark 4:38, KJV), but he also WEPT (John 11:35, KJV)!"

"Charity/love begins at home." (Sir Thomas Brown, English Theologian, 1642). "After God, your family is your first ministry. You cannot effectively care for others if you are not caring for yourself. Take time to relax, eat, and just get away." (Mark 6:31-32, NIV).

Folks will be mad that you are not at their beck and call, but it will teach them how to pray for you and not prey on you.

In May of 2016, one month after God called me to pastor my own church, my Godfather died in my home on Hospice. Only 4 folks out of a congregation of 300 came to the house to visit him before his death or visit me after his death. My Godfather had been a deacon in the church for more than 60 years. I'd been in various leadership roles in the same church for more than a decade! At his funeral, several of the congregants who expressed their love for both of us on numerous occasions, many of whom had put their feet under my table and wined and dined with me in my home as invited guests, came up and hugged me, greeted me with a Godly kiss on the cheek (Judas), and offered their condolences. I asked them why they didn't call or come to visit us. They seemed as surprised as a deer caught in headlights. They instantly began stumbling and stammering over their words and seemed suddenly incapable of making direct eye contact.

In a lame attempt to recover, they responded with "Um, well, um, weelll…I don't know. I'm not used to seeing you down or sad, and I didn't want to see him sick, but you know I love you and I'm here for you. If you need anything just give me a call."

"Skuurr" (sounds of tires screeching). I shook my head and

thought to myself, "Jesus take the wheel or stop the world so I can get off!" In the words of the late Barry White, "Mmhum, Sho You Right!" My head was reeling. I thought, "Call you?! I don't think so. My phone rings just as well as it dials! BYE FELICIA!"

"After [Judas had taken] the piece of bread, Satan entered him. Then Jesus said to him, 'What you are going to do, do quickly [without delay]." (John 13:27, Amplified Bible).

There can be no ascension without betrayal. You break bread together and even eat with them, but Judas still betrayed Christ and Peter denied him thrice.

THE SON

I met my son's father at age 14. He was 28. I got pregnant at 15 years old. Can we say statutory rape?

At age 16, I gave birth to my only begotten son, moved out of my mother's home, and began living with this abusive "baby daddy" who was 14 years my senior. Due to our age difference, his friends called him "Chester the Child Molester."

He was a small-time drug dealer and a self-proclaimed Five-Percenter in the Nation of Islam (NOI). Born and raised a Christian in the Baptist church, that "grown man" had my head messed up. I was going to the Mosque, reading the Quran, wearing turbans on my head, long sleeves, garments to my ankles to hide the bruises underneath, walking three feet behind him on the sidewalk with my head down, two black eyes, a busted lip, and the one who walked closest to the curb as "advertisement" in a skimpy tight-fitting outfit by night.

I was a straight-A student in school on the Principals' List every quarter of every year. I was President of my freshman and sophomore class. I was on the JV basketball team and Varsity Field Hockey Team. I was the Ambassador and spokesperson for my high school. I was a member of the Student Government Association and a candidate for the Jr. Honor Society. I loved to watch Jeopardy and

ALL THE PREACHER'S WIVES
A Peek Behind The Curtain Of Being A Preacher's Wife

Wheel of Fortune and could answer mostly all the questions and solve nearly all the puzzles. I was the top athlete in my gym class. My girlfriends in high school called me "Mama" because I was wise beyond my years and knew the names and symptoms of most illnesses and sexually transmitted diseases that plagued our generation in the '90s. I was raised in the church. My mom didn't send us to church she went to church with us.

I sang on the Youth choir, was Jr. Superintendent of the Sunday School, served on the Youth Usher Board, recited Easter speeches, sang with the family's singing group - The Washingtoneers, gave the welcome address in church every youth Sunday, and did public speaking engagements at various churches during Black History Month as early as the age of six.

What the heck happened?

What turned a good teenager into a problem child and made an innocent good kid turn seemingly hotter than a .45 that needed to be shot or a nickel box of matches that needed to be struck? Molestation and fondling at the hands of my mother's then-husband. The man she married after she and my father divorced. A man with the complexion connection and of the Caucasian persuasion-A White Man! Although I was born in the south in the 70s, I had never experienced slavery. After those ordeals, a spirit of bondage and promiscuity consumed me. I was bound by feelings of guilt, shame, hurt, confusion, despair, depression, disappointment, and thoughts of suicide. I just wanted to be free. Free to give my body away by choice, and not to have it taken away by his force.

As a pre-teen into my teenage years, I was worshipping in the House of the Lord on Sundays but was forbidden by him to speak about what was going on in our house Monday-Saturday when he was home. I have ALWAYS known my mother to be someone who worked tirelessly in the church and tithed faithfully to the ministry. She was at church every time the doors opened and twice on Sunday.

Unbeknownst to her, while she was at church being free and seeking God's face with the fruit of her lips; I was at home being held

ALL THE PREACHER'S WIVES
A Peek Behind The Curtain Of Being A Preacher's Wife

down, bound, and kissed on mine by her then-husband - the Man of Caucasian Persuasion. While she's in church, waving her hands, crying, and singing praises to the pillars; I am home kicking and fighting, being cornered, choked, and forced to scream into my pillow.

He was a long-distance truck driver. He transported goods across the U.S. via semi-truck. One night he took us on a ride in his big rig. In an attempt to scare us into keeping our mouths shut about the physical and sexual abuse, he began driving the rig recklessly on Route 40. As a result, the tractor-trailer jacked-knifed and crashed into the guardrail with us landing upside down in the passenger seat. Thanks to the late Deaconess Joann Mckoy, we were able to escape this nightmare and to finally speak about what we could not speak about for what seemed like forever but may have only been several painful months to a year.

Now, I was 16, pregnant with a child, and "grown." I was living with my baby daddy in an apartment that he and a roommate rented. In my mind, it was my own; and in the spirit of Kanye West, no one could "tell me nothing." In my young, dumb mind, this man was my biblical version of Boaz. After a year and a half of domestic abuse through pistol whippings, loaded guns shoved down my throat and aimed at my head, cuts, scrapes, burns, bruises, black eyes, busted lips, threats to kill me and our unborn son, and at 36 and a half weeks pregnant, suffering a literal stab wound by him using a Samurai Sword, I was finally done. The fact is had the blade gone 1.5 inches deeper and a little more to the left, it could have been fatal. While the women reading this are probably saying, "Oh My God, I'm so sorry this happened to you," there is somebody out there laughing and probably thinking to themselves, "Dang, sure didn't take much to leave, did it?" In the words of psalmist Kurt Carr, "I almost let go. I felt like I just couldn't take life anymore. The devil really had me, but Jesus came and grabbed me, and he held me close so I would let go. God's mercy kept me so I wouldn't let go."

How many of you know that prayer can go where you can't? Thanks be to God, I had a praying mother named, Ivory, and a friend, who had a praying Grandmother, named Apostle Glennie Burch. Although my mother may not have known where I was living because he had forbidden me to disclose our address or to say anything to anyone about the abuse, God knew right where to find me. Scripture says, "The effectual fervent prayers of the righteous availeth much." Through faith in God and the prayers of the righteous, I found the strength and courage to leave him.

I thank God for my high school teacher and basketball coach Corliss Johnson. Regardless of all I had been through, she never stopped looking at me as the same child she had always known. At the age of 16, I rededicated my life to Christ in the home of Corliss' parents, the late Clifford & Gertrude Johnson. Ms. Gertrude was also a member of Mount Pleasant Church & Ministries in Baltimore, Maryland. The pastor of the church was her son Bishop Clifford M. Johnson, Jr. I will never forget the day Ms. Gertrude anointed her frail caramel-colored hands with oil, laid those anointed hands upon my head, heart, stomach, and abdomen, and prayed a prayer of salvation over my life. Through that prayer, I felt the weight of the world lift off my shoulders. I saw myself as God would see me covered with the blood of Jesus, free from sin, guilt, and shame. Through that prayer, Ms. Gertrude Johnson strengthened me, uplifted my spirits, loved on me, embraced me, and hugged me so close I could feel her heart beating through my chest. She encouraged me to return to my first love, God.

After rededicating my life to Him, like the prodigal daughter, I came to myself. I immediately realized that the man that I thought was my Boaz was just an abusive-az, broke-az, no job having-az, lying-az, cheating-az, rape-az. I packed one bag, boarded a Greyhound bus, and took my baby and my black-az to Ft. Campbell, Kentucky to get away from him and live with my older sister, Stephanie, along with her military family.

"Walk with wise and become wise. For a companion of fools suffers harm." (Proverbs 13:20, NIV).

THE THREE AT 21

My sister worked on Sunday so there was no requirement for me to go to church regularly. I visited a few local congregations and was quickly reminded of what I'd come out of as a child. No thanks. Not interested. I was free to once again be "grown." Rather than worship in the house of the Lord, I would find myself at the local strip club, Kat West, seeking work. I had no desire to be a stripper. I wanted to be a server/waitress. I was told by some of the girls at the local convenience store that the military men that frequented the strip club tipped well. Because I was not yet 21, I couldn't work as a server because they served alcoholic beverages. However, because I was 18, I could dance/strip. THE DEVIL IS A LIAR! I can't bring beer or wine in a glass to someone at a table because I'm not 21, but I could bend over and wind my behind on a table at age 18?! Baby, I was born at night but not last night. I don't have to eat a whole cow or pig to know I'm eating beef or pork. This is some bologna! I didn't get the job as a server and refused the job as a stripper. I went from looking to work in adult male entertainment to the opposite end of the spectrum, childcare.

After 5 years of living in Kentucky, I would return to Baltimore with not only my son but now two daughters by two different men- a total of three children all with different fathers in different states. Can you say, "Hold up; wait a minute!" But God was not through with me yet.

"Being confident of this very thing, that he which hath begun a good work in you will perform it until the day of Jesus Christ:" (Philippians 1:6")

I was married at age 24. My then-husband and I took on the responsibility of raising 5 children: 4 girls and 1 boy, my 3 biological and his two biological children. At 24, I was a mother, wife, minister, full-time employee, and full-time college student. My family worshipped faithfully in the ministry where I served as a Minister and my then-husband played bass guitar. The children sang in the choir

ALL THE PREACHER'S WIVES
A Peek Behind The Curtain Of Being A Preacher's Wife

that I directed. Life was mostly good until it wasn't. After hearing the call to transfer our membership, we left this ministry and joined a larger congregation.

Moving to a much larger congregation, our blended family was quite a conversation piece for parishioners at our new place of worship. For example, during our meet and greet sessions, some folk would use that time to ask whose child belonged to whom because they didn't all have the same hair texture. They would also ask if my youngest child was bi-racial because her complexion was much lighter or whiter than that of the other children. They would compare the children to who they thought was prettiest based on their skin tone or the size of their noses or lips. Parishioners would boldly tell me that they had nicknames for my children such as Team White Meat, Team Dark Meat, or Team Peanut Butter. In earshot, some parishioners would comment on the shape of my curves or the size of my calves. They would jokingly say to one another, "The minister must be nuts" or did he simply enjoy having 3 children who were all different shades of brown. One parishioner even confessed to me that he would get an erection every time I stood to bring the Word of God just by the sound of my voice across the pulpit. I was still healing and working through my issues and past pain. I certainly wasn't trying to dig up old bones or pick at wounds that were slowly trying to heal.

The pastor of the church was made aware of all these happenings. He and his wife embraced my family and we become very close. He also became the Godfather of my youngest child, Stephanie, who is now 25 and a college graduate with multiple degrees. His wife became the Godmother of my middle daughter, Kinnidy, who is almost 27 and soon to graduate with a doctorate degree. Of course, my son Justin, who is almost 31, didn't allow any of it to faze him. He went on to college at Pennsylvania State University. While in college he recorded rap music that's on all the streaming platforms under the name "Oxygen Pernell." On Mother's Day 2014, my only begotten son, Justin, graduated from Pennsylvania State University with two degrees.

Through God and my children, I've been blessed with 3 handsome biological grandsons: Kamden, Karden, and Ronin. One

ALL THE PREACHER'S WIVES
A Peek Behind The Curtain Of Being A Preacher's Wife

bonus grandson, Lil Justin, and one granddaughter in love, Dior.

My ex and I remarried again in 2015 only to divorce four years later. Yes, I've been married three times but only to two different men because I was crazy enough to marry one of them twice!!! They say, "three strikes and you're out!" I'd like to think the third time is the charm.

In June of 2021, I married my now-husband, friend, confidant, king and covering within our ministry, Minister and Prophet "T". Through the grace of God, he understands how to love me and deal with my kind of crazy.

I endured all of this in my various roles in ministry while worshipping, working, and serving in the church as a progressive woman in ministry. I experienced real-life tragedies, traumas, triggers, and triumphs all while neglecting my own well-being and, at times, the needs of my family for the sake of the ministry.

Today, I will not wear a false smile on my face to disguise the hurt and pain in my heart. No more will I wear make-up or clothing for the sake of concealing the wounds of people stabbing me in the back. No more will I wear the blame, guilt, and shame of trying to clean up what people refuse to admit they've messed up. I've made up my mind that I will always lift up the name of Jesus and Bless the Lord and allow His praise, and not pain, to fill my mouth. You're reading about a woman who eventually cried, threw her hands up, and said - I GIVE UP! Now, I throw my hands up, not in anger, frustration, or aggravation, but in praise, thanksgiving, and adoration. Thankfully, I He gave me the courage not to give up on life but to surrender to Him. Today, I give it all to God!

So, if you are ever feeling down or lost and you find yourself questioning God's love for you, remember me and my story. By the grace of God, I have disrobed and still, God continues to love this stripper, me, Dorothy Henley.

ALL THE PREACHER'S WIVES
A Peek Behind The Curtain Of Being A Preacher's Wife

Liza Hines

"People always think it's glitz and glam but, when I really sat and thought about how I really felt, the words that kept ringing in the back of my mind were "punching bag!"

ALL THE PREACHER'S WIVES
A Peek Behind The Curtain Of Being A Preacher's Wife

2
You are Stronger Than You Think

When people know that you are the wife of a pastor, the first question they all want to know is "what is it like?" I never know what to say because you want to be truthful but you also wanna say it the right way. People always think it's glitz and glam but, when I really sat and thought about how I really felt the words that kept ringing in the back of my mind were punching bag! Do not you dare laugh that is how it feels. People with their outrageous requests, their snooty looks, and how they disregard you at times…yeah, a punching bag is the perfect way to describe it. Just stand there look pretty and take it because the call on your husband's life is great. What about me? What about my family?

I remember when I was growing up it seemed like the pastor's wife was seen and not too much heard from. As a child, I always thought they were being ladylike, poised, and feminine but when I became one I realized they were doing all they could to hold their tongue, keep the peace, protect their families, and stay saved child! Whew, God knows all things. You cannot tell me the Bible doesn't have all that we need in it to live because Paul was spot on when he gave the instructions to crucify our flesh daily. I like how it says it in the Message version

ALL THE PREACHER'S WIVES
A Peek Behind The Curtain Of Being A Preacher's Wife

Galations 5:24, "..Among those who belong to Christ, everything connected with getting our own way and mindlessly responding to what everyone else calls necessities is killed off for good---crucified." I really considered that. When I did, I realized that I had gone into this position thinking about the wrong things and in doing so I was getting frustrated, sad at times, and allowing myself to be overwhelmed. I had to come to the realization that if I was going to do this and keep myself intact something had to give! I needed some tools to keep that flesh subjected. It appears I was given all types of opportunities for the flesh to rear its ugly head and if I did not yield to those inner SOS moments, I was afraid of what may have happened. Which again takes me back to the punching bag. We will get into that more later… I know you are wondering (like myself at the time) how did I even get to this place?

Well, most pastors start a church (feel led by God to go out find a building, logo, mission/vision and gather members) and some pastors are planted in a church (a church getting its existence from an existing church where things are already in place). My husband and I pastored a church that was planted. We took on the responsibility of this church after the pastors moved to another state to plant a new one. When we started a lot of the directions and meetings were held with my husband and though I was invited to sit in on them it was very evident that no one was talking to me. It was a red flag moment that I kinda pushed aside because this was an opportunity to support my husband as we serve God. Who wants to be the wife who gets all these checks in the spirit and acts on them? I did not want to bog my husband down with that mild concern, so I just pushed it down within myself. I had no idea how much space a woman has to store mixed emotions, frustrations, and confusion within herself. I will say my husband always tried to assure me that we were a team in this yes decision! I would find subtle ways to remind him too as we journeyed through ministry as pastors now that we are a team, right? We took this responsibility very serious, and we wanted to do it right as much as we could. We understand that how we treated each other and how we treated the congregation was very important, but we had to remain a team. There would be times

ALL THE PREACHER'S WIVES
A Peek Behind The Curtain Of Being A Preacher's Wife

where it felt like others advice to him would be that he is the head and in control and he did not need my opinion. There would be other times when it was unspoken but loudly heard that he was the pastor, and I should kinda separate myself and my children when in church settings by people. That was another flag moment that I quietly despised but, forced downward within myself as to stay in my place so to speak. I started to think this cannot be healthy for me. How much can one person tolerate and for how long?

As you can see of these questions were starting to become a part of me and this was only the beginning. I started to hear in the back of my mind a lot 1 Peter 5:6-7 MSG, "So be content with who you are, and don't put on airs. God's strong hand is on you; he will promote you at the right time. Live carefree before God; He is most careful with you. You know that same scripture as "cast your cares on Him because He cares for you. If you are anything like me, I sometimes choose what I want to concern God with. Not like I'm hiding things from Him, but I often consider all the things He has to do in a day then decide if I want to add this little thing to His plate. So, I am always rethinking my prayers saying let me just pray about part of this or I can do that I just need a little help but subconsciously not casting the care just kinda talking to God about it from time to time all the while stuffing myself with the very cares that Jesus died on the cross for so I wouldn't have to worry about. I mean if I can handle it why bring it to Jesus at all. Either trust Him or don't. Why do we do that? I honestly felt like the emotions I had were sometimes petty and insignificant in comparison to all the cancer, natural disasters, and addictions that God needed to handle and here I am with hurt feelings, feelings of defeat, and struggling to keep my happy demeanor. I had somehow forgotten that big or small God cares about every part of me. He feels the same way about you. I was working so hard to make sure ministry continued and making sure I was there in any way my husband may need for me to be that I was once again brought back to the thoughts of how much can one person hold and tolerate for how long? Ringing even louder was what should I do… I NEED TOOLS! I just knew that there was

ALL THE PREACHER'S WIVES
A Peek Behind The Curtain Of Being A Preacher's Wife

something that I was missing but what?

My mom was not a pastor's wife. I was not raised in a home where I was groomed to marry a pastor or minister. I was really boggled by what was now happening in my life. Ministry had become my life in a whole different way. I mean I grew up in ministry. My mom was over the usher board and the anniversary committees when I was a kid. My aunts and uncles were pastors. I sang in the youth choir, danced on the dance team, and worked in youth ministry but I had never been a pastor. It hit me one day that I did marry a man who knew from when we were kids that he would work in ministry so what's the problem? Early on his plan was to be an evangelist so he went to college, and he sharpened his tools to do that. I had prepared for that not this. While he was out preaching his mom would speak into me when we'd go to support him or just in general. I prayed that God would bring back to my remembrance those things my mom-in-love Corener Hines had spoken to me when I was a young unmarried girl and then again as a married woman because I sure could use them. I needed those things that I'd put on the top shelf or even accidentally thrown out because I had no plans of being a pastor's wife. She said, "you may not want to be a pastor's wife, but your husband will pastor one day." I'd say, "noooo don't speak that into my life." We would laugh. It wasn't that I didn't see the honor in it, but I was just that. I did. I saw the honor in it and knew how God saw the call. There is so much responsibility with being a pastor. It's more than preaching messages and nice suits. It is paying the bills, it's keeping the building up to code, building partnerships with the community, and most importantly it's about souls. Our Bishop Darrell always said, "the church isn't his, the people belong to God." So, whenever you're handling God's people you have to do it a certain way. As a kid, I just felt like that is a lot of responsibility on 1-2 people. I felt compassion towards the pastors because of the load they carry. So, I tried to just lie down and try to recall those old conversations. She was a pastor's wife for more than 25 years. She would tell me things like "women will always throw themselves at your husband but, don't let that bother you because your husband chose

ALL THE PREACHER'S WIVES
A Peek Behind The Curtain Of Being A Preacher's Wife

you." She'd also say, "you are your husband's peace, make sure you are prayerful so when he needs to come to you, he finds refuge with you. Don't make it worse for him when he comes home." As I started to recall these things it made me feel calmer and it strengthened me. I thought to myself this is just what I need. I kept on thinking about other advice or words that I could lean on. I didn't want us to survive ministry, but I wanted us to thrive in ministry. I wanted to serve in excellence alongside my husband. I had to come up with a strategy!

1. I needed a squad.

Mother Hines was part of the squad way before I needed it. The wisdom I had held onto had given me the spark I needed. After reminiscing it became evident to me that if I wasn't going to completely share these with my husband or God these feelings, I was having then I needed to find someone to confide in like a go-to squad. I asked God to send me a group or show me a group that I can go to. I asked God for them to be trustworthy and for them to be open to mentoring me. After a while, I reached out to some women that I knew and had connected with before and some of them I didn't know but I could aspire to be like them. It couldn't be based on superficial things like looks, followers, and possessions but as I started to watch how they interacted with their husbands and church members I knew it had to be based on the inside, their character. I wanted to be able to pray with them and we needed to be able to uplift each other. I also needed to be able to be myself with them even if that meant being vulnerable because when you are not honest and humble how can you expect to get the help you seek?

There was an incident that happened at the church that really upset me. I'm very straightforward and by the book. I am a stickler for the rules. There was a time when I asked a member not to do something because of liability issues. Instead of the member understanding my heart and my concerns it turned into a power struggle. A lot of things were said to me that didn't sit well with me. I was trying to get the person to understand I was just doing my job in essence and that I wasn't trying to exert power, but I know we were responsible for the space, so I wanted to make sure everything was done in order. My husband ended up handling it but, I couldn't shake how I felt. It didn't have to be that way. I tried to explain to my husband how I was feeling (he is a great listener) but I needed to get these feelings to a squad member. I called my sister Pastor Pamela. I told her I need to just say it as I felt it. She said okay let me get somewhere that I can hear it and respond. I told her what happened, and she listened all the way to the end. When I finished explaining, she said, "Liza don't let anyone, or anything disturb your peace. Your husband and your children are your responsibility, you have a duty to them. Do what you feel led to do and then stop when you feel the need to stop. People will destroy your peace if you let them. Don't let them." I knew at that moment I could wash my hands of that moment and move on. So, I did. Oh yeah, the squad isn't for everything they're for certain things. They are the secret weapon. They do not replace God they're a necessary part of the toolbox. This isn't the regular group of friends. This isn't even people you'd normally hang with. Stretch yourself. These people will mature you, encourage you, and cause you to reflect and grow. You and God need to choose the squad.

2. **Protect your children at all costs.**

I know what you are thinking, "what do you mean it's church, what's the least that could happen?" Well, I grew up with tons of PKs (pastor's kids) and you probably know some too. You know a lot of times they were doing all the stuff the pastor preached to us not to do so. They were also the kids that you grew up with wishing there was something you could've said or done to help steer them in the right direction. They are often the kids that grow up and resent church and God. My husband and I tried to avoid that. So, we decided that if the two of us were a team, then we needed the whole team. We call ourselves the Fab4. We had meetings with just the four of us and we'd ask their opinions and ask what they thought about service and the church. Once again, another defaulted yes. The kids were there as a result of the yes, their parents gave. As we drove two hours there and sometimes 2 ½ hours back each Sunday (depending on if the Packers were playing or the weather it could take longer) the kids grew weary in well doing. I noticed it when my daughter magically wanted to stay the night with my mom every Saturday. My son one time said, "hey it's not fair that she gets to skip church! I don't want to take this long drive either." I had not thought about it like that until that moment. Here I thought it was cute that she wanted to spend all this extra time with her grandma and here it was she had tricked me. ☺ When we got home, I called a family meeting. We sat the kids down and flat out said to our daughter, "are you staying the night at grandma's house to avoid going to church?" She looked sad at first and then she smiled saying, "yes, it's too long to get there. We stay too long afterward and there aren't a lot of kids' things to do or kids." Dang, well tell us how you really feel I thought but I respected her voice and let's be real I asked her. There were tons of adults with few children, especially their age group. I get it. After our meeting, my husband and I took that info and he said, "no kids really like church." I felt a check within me that stood up to say wait! It was important that our kids were heard. It was then I said to my husband, "That's true but wait. I will not sacrifice our children for ministry. This is valuable information. We need to grow from it." I did not want them to confuse church work with God. God is God. The work and the gathering are a part of serving but they are just that. We grew up in a time where they prided themselves on "doing what our hands find to do" staying late and eating calling it ministry because this was being done at church. I'm not saying it's not good to work hard in ministry. I'm just saying sometimes it's too much and it's too much for everyone. Since Jesus cares so much about the children and what they say then we should to. What sense does it make to preach these prolific words and bring Jesus to so many and miss your own household? Make it make sense, right? Once the children felt like they were a part of it all they took ownership and started helping.

3. Find your place in ministry, bring something of substance to offer.

I wanted to dispel the trophy-wife myth. Not saying that's what I was, I'm just referring to the beginning where women were seen and not heard. After I felt like I didn't have a strong voice I started to wonder what my place was there. I didn't want to start going through the motions and I didn't want to stop going. I started asking God to show me what I needed to be doing. I didn't want to cause conflict in my home but, I just felt like I needed more, like I could be doing more. I kept hearing people call me "First Lady" so then it made me think of how I wanted to be more than a pretty face. Who will they say I am? Ya know? My mother told me, "If people are concerned with how, you look then their priorities are off. You need to make sure you are just trying to show off the word and godliness." I also remember my spiritual mom Joyce Tucker telling me, "You are enough. You are good enough. I love that you are never the change the essence of who you are. Don't let that go." I had to shift my focus to the heart and not look the part. I've always had my own version of fashion anyways. I can look good and dress nice but if the inside doesn't match the outside, what is the point? I stopped sitting pretty and I got more involved. I felt a tug in my heart for the community. I talked to my husband, and we agreed that we wanted to gain a presence in the community we pastored in. I love people and I love to help others, so I hosted a Bible drive. We collected 75 Bibles to be handed out as we went door to door with the church inviting the community to our church. My husband even added the element of prayer, so we prayed too with those who would allow us to. I helped him host a monthly food drive where we fed 30 families' groceries a month. Then we hosted an outdoor service. We grilled out, gave away school supplies, and preached the gospel with a DJ! The mayor even came out! It really gave me more of a purpose and further let us know that ministry is more than the four walls. I was not trying to prove myself, but it caused them to see me differently. It also helped the members get more involved and they started to look for more opportunities to do so. When your heart starts to look more like God's heart, your connection to the ministry comes alive.

4. You are a team.

No matter what happens or what comes your way you and your husband are on the same team. It may not always feel like it because his thoughts are one-sided at times only for the church and you see the big picture with the church included. No matter what do not let anything divide the bond you have built. Like any team, everyone

ALL THE PREACHER'S WIVES
A Peek Behind The Curtain Of Being A Preacher's Wife

involved needs to bring their gifts, compassion, empathy, one goal, and enthusiasm every time knowing that you are two people working towards the same goal. You both must build the foundation. You both have to remember the vision and mission. You both must find a balance. It cannot always be about the ministry. Do not forget date nights and private meeting times just to be together without the pressure of ministry is just as important if not more. Make sure you have not given a 100% to the ministry and saved the scraps for your spouse and children. There must be a balance. You are a team. When there are systems and plans in place the team can work harmoniously. When ministry is done there's still the two of you and your family make sure you have a firm foundation.

These top four things shifted my focus tremendously! My squad is still growing. We are a stronger unit. Finding my place allowed personal growth too. Our kids are older and they're finding their own ways to serve in ministry.

I know you are thinking get to the point… why the punching bag? Well, think about it what is a punching bag?

A punching bag is a sturdy bag designed to repeatedly withstand punches. It is cylinder-shaped and filled with materials that cause the bag to be hardened. I couldn't figure out how to start this piece but every time I asked myself what it is like to be a pastor's wife those two words kept coming up and blinking like a neon light. Punching bags are often found in a gym or sports environment, not church right? They can be associated with stress relief and or fighting or preparation. I thought it was harsh to compare myself or other women to a punching bag because it sounds weird. The more I read about punching bags the more I understood the benefits of a punching bag. It strengthens your core and brings stability, improves coordination, and builds stamina and endurance. So, what are you saying Liza, I'm a punching bag deal with it. No, I'm not saying that at all. We are not punching bags per se. I would never encourage you to be one physically or emotionally either. I'm just saying doesn't it seem like it sometimes though? With all that the punching bag goes through it still stands and still serves its purpose. As the pastor's wife sometimes, we must endure these hard things for the sake of ministry and in support of our husbands but at the end of the day, we are still standing sturdy and strengthened to serve. Even Jesus endured the cross and disregarded the shame attached to it for our sake. Jesus didn't end on the cross though and every stripe, blow or hit that he took brought us to where we are now and for eternity. No, we are not Jesus either. We ARE created in His image and in His likeness. So, I encourage you when you have those punching bag moments girl get the squad on the line, adjust your focus to remember it's bigger than you, find those kids let them encourage you, and let bae know ya need to meet up so you can pull it back together. You are so needed in your life, in your home, in the lives of your family, and in the ministry you both pastor. The punching bag endures a lot but, once it swings back into its position it benefits everyone it encounters. Let me leave this scripture to encourage you in Hebrews 12:2, "…we do this by keeping our eyes on Jesus the champion who initiates and perfects our faith because of the joy awaiting him." Ladies as we stand alongside our husbands remember with all our tools, we still look to Jesus who is the perfect example that there's hope and we too can reach the goal that is set before us. You are stronger than you think.

Dr. Velma Bagby

"The usher led me to a seat in the audience. After they introduced me, rather than lead me to the pulpit, the usher led me to the front of the church. They placed a small stand there, which looked like it was designed to hold sheet music."

ALL THE PREACHER'S WIVES
A Peek Behind The Curtain Of Being A Preacher's Wife

3
Praise God Anyhow

I had forewarning about the difficulties and the drama that can arise surrounding the role of a pastor's wife thanks to the multiple experiences I witnessed of women who served in this role. In one denomination, I witnessed what happens when members dislike the pastor's wife. How the church board acted inappropriately towards the couple. Eventually, the two divorced.

Yet in another case, I saw the pastor's wife show disdain for a family member of mine. She disliked the fact that her husband, the pastor, assigned the family member as choir director rather than her. My family member continued to show respect toward them both, even though the pastor's wife made it obvious to everyone that she hated the decision.

The third story I witnessed was the preacher's wife experiencing abuse within the marriage. I thought it odd that the members ignored the behavior they saw. The pastor's wife looked sad most of the time, and my heart ached to witness behavior contrary to loving a wife "like Christ loves the church." Even more difficult was when she dismissed efforts to comfort her.

Then, there's my personal experience. One pastor called me into a meeting and berated my service on the praise team. He told me I wasn't a good fit for the team, and that I should step down. Of course, I wanted to know why he was saying this. He had no direct reason or specific example. Instead, he became agitated and raised his voice saying, "I want you to step down." I remember he referenced me having a Jezebel spirit. I served on the praise team, taught in the school of ministry, and conducted Bible study in the women's ministry. When he used those hurtful words to question my reputation on the praise team, I responded that if his report was true, it should apply to all my areas of service. So, I stepped down from all of them. My response shocked him. It upset me, but I remained respectful. Shaking inside, I could not wait to tell my husband. After I spoke with my husband, he met with that pastor and advised him not to meet with me in private unless he was present. I was proud of my husband and felt his protection. We later discovered that the reason the pastor asked me to step down from the praise team was that another member wanted to replace me. We soon left that ministry.

  Having grown up in church, being active in a variety of roles, allowed me to get to know some of the drama behind the curtain during most of my adult Christian life—what the congregation does not see. Seeing it prepared me for some of the drama I could expect in my leadership role and helped me guard against it. My husband and I joke about our experiences and say, "Well, now we know what not to do."

  During my formative years as a Christian young adult, I watched preachers' wives who were ignored, misjudged, abused in their marriages, and sometimes mistreated at the hands of members. I also witnessed preachers' wives acting as if they were superior to their fellow preachers' wives. I've yet to discover the purpose of that behavior. I often wondered if the larger ministries saw themselves as superior to the smaller ones.

  Before becoming a preacher's wife, I suffered discrimination in some denominations that did not support female ministers/preachers—even though I was an ordained minister with a Doctorate in Theology. They didn't care. I recall when a local church invited me to speak. The usher led me to a seat in the audience. After they introduced me, rather than lead me to the pulpit, the usher led me to the front of the church. They placed a small stand there, which looked like it was designed to hold sheet music. As I placed my Bible on the stand, in my heart I said Lord, "I'll preach wherever you send me." The message was on fire. Afterward, the pastor approached me and said, "You might change my mind about female preachers."

Another occasion happened when my dad passed away and I was the speaker. To secure a larger church, my brother called a local pastor to inquire about using his facility. The pastor told my brother he would not allow me in the pulpit. Thankfully, our ministry was in a building because we decided not to worry about whether there was room for everyone, as long as my family had space. I felt free to preach what God had given me. Again, God sent fire through the message. Afterward, the minister of that other church came up to me and acknowledged the powerful message.

Having gone through the storms and witnessing the travesty of how women were treated in ministry, I realized it was all part of my preparation. I did not take the discriminatory practices personally, but kept my focus on God, on winning souls, ministering to those who were less fortunate, and inspiring as well as encouraging fellow followers of Jesus Christ.

The drama I witnessed growing up, and the discriminatory practices towards women, including myself, prepared me to manage my role as a preacher's wife with grace. I am always friendly but recognizing being friendly wasn't always welcomed. I remember meeting a young preacher's wife at a conference. I was aware they had recently moved to the area, and I had not had a chance to meet them. I greeted the wife and said, "Hi, our church ministries are in the same area. I'm glad to meet you." She looked at me and snapped, "Oh, so you had to wait to get to the conference to meet me?" She walked away. Her rude behavior shocked me. Some of her members assured me it wasn't me, but she had the problem. I dismissed the behavior and asked God to help me never to be like what I witnessed.

I've gone to other events and gatherings, and the treatment is the same. Unless you're of a notable ministry, you're not included in the group. Our ministry is small. And our focus was never on building notoriety but on doing God's work.

ALL THE PREACHER'S WIVES
A Peek Behind The Curtain Of Being A Preacher's Wife

***

My husband and I both attended church as a youth. But because we were young when we accepted Christ and did not live our lives as believers, we both recommitted our lives to the Lord as adults and were re-baptized: me at the age of 24, and him at 35.

By the time we were called to be servant leaders, we were both 58 years old and had been married 38 years. Now married for 48 years, we have been leaders for the past 10 years. Three of the 10 years we spent conducting ministry online. Thankfully, the landlord released us from our lease, during the preliminary stages of the pandemic.

It is important to build and maintain a solid relationship with your husband and I am fortunate because the Lord saw fit to call my husband to an assistant pastor, then later to plant a church after 38 years of marriage and our girls were adults.

But, before planting a church, as we prepared to leave the last ministry, we were in great company because our friend, Minister Dansby joined us. She was a dear friend, my sidekick in the pulpit, one of the pastor's two associate ministers, and one of our greatest supporters. She always had our backs. God blessed us with a jewel by our side. She was an avid prayer warrior, helper, and preacher, and could slay demons while ministering to people at the altar. It came as a shock when the Lord took her home last year. Although I did not feel any loneliness in my role, I felt a void missing a trusted friend.

As we planted the ministry, we were determined to approach our role with integrity. We were transparent with our members. They embraced us and loved us because of it. We earned their respect. The beautiful way the members embraced and treated us both blessed me; I could feel their love and respect for us both.

When we hit those rough patches on our journey, there is a phrase I choose to use concerning my response, *"I'm not in high school anymore."* In high school, we reacted to everything and responded to every comment. God expects us to follow his instructions in the face of challenges, and I choose to do it his way.

There is also a graphic of this very point circulating on Facebook, and it provides the perfect visual of my point. The sheet of

ALL THE PREACHER'S WIVES
A Peek Behind The Curtain Of Being A Preacher's Wife

paper has a large circle in the middle and inside the circle is the title, "In My Control," and the words: my thoughts, actions, how I speak, handle challenges, and boundaries. Outside of the circle has the title "Out of My Control'," with the words: actions of others, the past, opinions of others, happenings around me, future, what others do, and what people think of me. It's important to remember we serve God in our assignment; and whatever things we do, we do it for his glory. Again, I prefer to keep my blessings flowing and fight to not allow outside influences to disrupt that flow.

Even though a board manages the operations of the church as an entity, what a husband and wife does as a couple must function as a team or as its own board. "A threefold cord cannot be broken." There's no "I" in the team. Neither are there more than two of you making those decisions. God made it clear to the very first couple to cleave only unto each other. Do not confuse your assignment in the ministry with your mandate in your marriage.

We left ministries because of the disparities and unfairness we saw from broken leadership examples. The story of Judas on the team with Jesus is our reminder that the enemy of your soul is lurking to see how and when he can tear down God's purpose for you. Guard and protect each other from the true enemy. My husband and I remind each other regularly, we are not enemies of each other. It is not flesh and blood. Although we would like to put a face to problems, the Bible tells us otherwise. Prioritize your assignment, but do not neglect your marriage and family.

I respect and support my husband in his role as pastor, as he does for me as a minister and preacher's wife. I understand what he faces and I'm no stranger to leadership principles or practices. In my role as a Deputy Administrator in the State government, I provided leadership to over 100 managers and staff and oversaw ten employment centers and multiple programs. I retired after working for 35 years. I had retired when we began to plant a church. My job trained and prepared me as a leadership expert. When I look back on what I witnessed growing up in the church compared to what I see today, it's absurd because I can still see the irregularities in how ministries continue to run.

It is important to learn how to separate church ministry from your home life. After work, when I walked into the door of our home, I returned to being my husband Bruce's wife and grandma to my grandkids. I did not bring my job title as Deputy Administrator home with me. My husband and I laugh about the fact that we are both preachers. However, when we are home, neither of us is looking for a preached word, but support and love. We both try to show that respect to each other and ensure we are sowing into our marriage ministry and home life. It can be as simple as picking up movie popcorn on the way home from church or shutting off our phones for a movie together. Sometimes it's riding to our favorite spot to grab a bite or a Starbucks blended drink or coffee. Figure out something but make a conscious effort each week to show love and spend some time with each other. One of our favorite things to do is grab snacks and coffee. We sit outside on our front porch and chat as we watch the sunset.

* * *

Although our church ministry is now 10 years old, and we spent 7 of those years in a building pre-pandemic. The recent 3, post the pandemic, have been online services. We have a congregation of under 50 members, and compared to many other ministries in our area, we are small.

What I love about being a servant leader is remembering that the people God sends belong to Him, and our job is to ensure that we are providing them with what they need to grow in their relationship with Him and to help them discover the call upon their lives. Our heart is to help more people follow Jesus, not just attend church.

I remember when we began our journey. We prayed for God to use us and started holding Sunday service in our living room. A few people joined our fellowship. Some told us they did not have a church home and were waiting for us to begin a church. As we remained in prayer, God sent word that we will get a building, and "it would be as simple as handing us the keys." When that moment came, a friend was vacating a building and asked us to take over his lease. He handed us the keys, and we later entered our lease with the church that managed the building. We were in awe of what God did.

In the beginning, our membership grew into a small congregation. Soon, several of our family members joined us. Our siblings wanted to walk with us and provide a source of comfort for us and confirmation we were on the right track. Family love blessed us.

As we got busy, help arrived to relieve me of some of my duties, and the two of us chose my husband's assistant. She is a sweet senior member of our church and loved both of us. Although a preacher's wife, it was important for my husband to include me in the decisions. At the same time, it also meant I was present in the experience with him and showed my interest in planting a successful ministry as his partner.

In ministry, we established a practice where my husband did not minister to women in private but ensured I was present. We knew of accusations that some leaders crossed the line when they were alone with a female member, and we wanted to avoid any appearance of inappropriateness. This added a layer of wisdom and safety.

In those cases where we addressed inappropriate women, I helped protect my husband from them. I can identify inappropriate behavior, even when it is subtle and appears innocent on the surface. Women know the antics of other women. All of it is an attack of the enemy. I'm reminded of two occurrences where my husband and I had to address disrespectful women.

In one situation, my husband did not question the behavior of a woman in a prior ministry, but I saw her antics. The woman acted flirtatiously when she addressed my husband, who was an assistant pastor. The way she interacted with him was more casual and less respectful than her interactions with the senior pastor. I brought her behavior to his attention immediately. It wasn't from a place of jealousy because our relationship was solid, but it came from a place of protection and ensuring that I covered my husband. He trusted my assessment and agreed. At the end of our conversation, I remember asking, "Do you want to handle this, or should I?" My husband

ALL THE PREACHER'S WIVES
A Peek Behind The Curtain Of Being A Preacher's Wife

responded he would take care of it. This woman oversaw the finances of the church, so whenever my husband purchased items for the church occasionally, she provided a check for reimbursement. My next exchange with the woman came when she approached me after church and said, "Minister Bagby said I should give you his checks from now on." I grinned and said, "Okay, thank you." I chuckled inside thinking, *Well, I guess my husband handled it.* She never showed that behavior towards him again. Laughing out loud.

There was a second occurrence, which took place after we began our ministry. A strange woman was visiting one Sunday. During the altar call, she purposely tried to avoid getting in the prayer line with Associate Minister Dansby (our other female minister) or my line and tried to get to my husband, who was busy ministering to the brothers. Both Minister Dansby and I saw her efforts and moved to shield my husband, so we forced this woman into one of our prayer lines. When the woman saw this, she turned and walked back to her seat. We also noticed her hanging around outside of the church once the service was over. This woman's curious behavior alerted the brothers, me, and several members. We all stayed behind after service to accompany the pastor when he left the building. It's for this reason, my husband and I established a policy that the two associate ministers prayed for the women and the pastor ministered to the men during the altar call.

Being a servant leader isn't about the glamor. There is nothing glamorous about this assignment. We're in it to serve. Focusing on the glamor makes me think of the state of the church when Jesus arrived. I'm not bigger, higher, or better than anyone Jesus charges us to serve. If it wasn't glamorous for Jesus, what makes us think it will be for us? He rejected the church of his time for glamorizing their role and building enormous homes for themselves, while the people suffered in poverty.

I recall watching other ministries struggle with their finances, but the leader continued taking a salary. When we faced similar challenges, my husband decided not to take a salary for a season. He wanted to give the ministry room to grow financially. Our membership comprised families at various financial levels, and we considered those with modest means of support to the ministry. It didn't seem fair to ask them to support us when we both had successful careers. Although I had already retired from the state government, and my husband continued working, we had a sufficient income.

After discussing it together, we agreed to the decision. Then my husband shared his preference not to take a salary with the church board. Surprised, the board saw his heart in that decision and appreciated him for it. Everyone in our ministry understood his choice, so they tried to make up for it by showering him with appreciation during special celebrations for him. The members also saw our hearts in terms of our role as servant leaders. They knew our ministry focus was on the spiritual growth of each member, helping the less fortunate through serving meals, clothing giveaways, and by giving away winter coats to school-aged children. We were also collecting designer purses filled with toiletries for the women at the shelter and so much more. All these things showed where we placed our ministry focus, and even the members who were struggling benefited as well.

Being a servant leader is not always sunshine and tiptoeing through the tulips. It is more of getting your feet and nails dirty, and sometimes skipping nail appointments in favor of the budget. It's about relinquishing the hats and suits and preferring to dress casually because the membership base we served could not afford it. I never hoped to present myself as if I was higher than or better than the people God chose us to serve.

Here are a few attributes you will need in your role as a servant leader with your husband: have a strong relationship with Jesus (if not now, grow it); build a strong marriage (marriage is your ministry); maintain a consistent prayer life (for yourself, your husband, as a couple or family, the ministry work, the people); be well-versed in the Word. It is your guide; practice love as described in the Word (how to love, who to love, what love is and is not); apply grace in every situation (be forgiving of yourself, your husband, and others); be resilient (this assignment is not for the weak); know when to be silent (it's a strength and the word silent and listen uses the same letters); practice good self-worth (build yourself, exercise self-care, take time out for you), have strong faith (trust God's leading in everything); be determined (you have a purpose, stay the course and do not give up); keep a tribe of supporters (use your family to fill the void of friendships). All of this helps you to weather the storms sometimes faced when dealing with an ungodly and unfriendly environment.

Prayer is key to building a solid marriage ministry. Pray daily together and for one another. Let nothing disrupt your pattern to pray for each other, family, ministry, decisions, and more. Praying and studying together create special moments and will help to maintain your bond.

Agreement is important — "How can two walk together unless they agree." Discuss details of decisions in the privacy of your own home, then agree to the approach together.

As a couple, recognize each of your strengths and use them. My husband comes to me for anything related to technology, or a business decision he must make. My husband is a financial wizard, that's his strength. We approach the decision together and once he is clear on the direction; he thanks me for my contribution and moves forward. Communicate to ensure you are both on the same page at home and then while at church, when your husband executes the decision. At least you know the two of you talked about it first.

Protect each other from harm—not every person who enters the building has your best interest at heart—those above or below your status. This can be tricky, but what's important is that you decide together how you wish to oversee the issues that arise at the church—especially those that impact you and your family.

* * *

Today, people are surprised at how long we have been married. We married at the age of twenty and recently celebrated 48 blessed years together. I can only credit God for that. Because of what we've both seen and witnessed, we set out to help other couples as well. We have ministered to many who were members of other ministries. We've provided singles and marriage counseling for couples who hit a rough patch. I've seen couples come for pre-marriage counseling hoping we could fix their problems, when the real problem was, they were marrying the wrong person. Witnessing this often and seeing some of the other problems repeat, remain with me.

I'm a firm believer that God has purpose on the other side of pain and difficulties. That purpose for me manifested in writing books that encourage women on their journey of discovering the mate they deserve and to bring back to the forefront God's date for marriage plan. It is thousands of years old versus the one we use today, which is a little over 100 years old. Churches tell singles to get married, but do not prepare them or counsel them on the topic. I've met many women and seen several tragedies on the news, from toxic relationships that could have been avoided had they been prepared better. The divorce rate in the church is just as high as in the world. Yet, believers are the ones given *"the keys to the kingdom."* Yet so many believers do not know about the keys or have forgotten how to use them.

All my journey has led me to what God wanted to birth out of my experiences while in my position as a preacher's wife. Our role is not only to be a partner to our husbands, but we are also spiritual mothers in the ministry. As a senior woman, the Bible tells me to "teach the younger." My heart now is to help other Christian women practice dating in a healthy way with a "date with intent" strategy. It is time to bring this level of training and preparation back. I hope to encourage others to pick up their keys.

ALL THE PREACHER'S WIVES
A Peek Behind The Curtain Of Being A Preacher's Wife

Author Melanie "The Voice" Johnson

"Even in the whispers and secret discussions, they gave us our space but made it clear – they didn't want anything to do with what we were doing."

ALL THE PREACHER'S WIVES
A Peek Behind The Curtain Of Being A Preacher's Wife

4
Relationship with the Master

"I've been called to preach." That is what he told me. What? By whom? When did this happen? I was not prepared for this. I had no idea that this was even a possibility. Nevertheless, here it was. He was announcing his calling into the ministry. What did that mean for me? Where would I fit in? Did this mean I was called too? But I hadn't heard anything. Was I listening to the right source? My life was filled with so many questions and who could answer them? I pondered over this new declaration. Could I be dreaming?

Don't get me wrong, I was completely involved in the church and the working of the Lord's mission. I had been raised in the Baptist church, but since my marriage began nine years prior, I had worshiped with Presbyterians, Southern Baptists, and United Methodists. So, I loved church, and I valued my relationship with God. Nevertheless, as with any 30-year-old, my husband and I had been enjoying life, having fun, and this was not what I pictured life in the ministry to be. It sent me into a depressive state. What would change about our lives? Was fun (card playing, social events, comedy shows, etc.) now out of the picture? Would our lives be consumed with the church, Bible study, and special programs? Still so many questions. Fewer answers.

Another drawback I had was being intimate with the pastor. I grew up thinking as a pastor being the closest thing to God on Earth. I could not think of a pastor in an intimate setting. Now that the pastor could be my husband, how would this work out? How could I separate the two? Should I separate the two? This may seem like a trivial question. Of course, we had been married for almost ten years, why would intimacy be an issue now? Well, there is more to this story...

I am a survivor of domestic abuse. I was only physically abused once in our first year of marriage, but the mental, emotional, and financial abuse began shortly after year two. So, here at nine years into the marriage, I had questions about how God could "call" someone who treated their spouse in such a manner. I wanted to ask that question, but who would I ask it to? I was reared believing you are not to question God. Was it really God who was calling? Why was I living in such turmoil with someone who was sent to lead a flock? God, I had so many questions and no one to turn to for answers. At least I thought I didn't.

Here I was. A young woman supporting her husband in every endeavor. I assisted him in his college courses and helped him get his advanced degrees. I assisted him in his career work as an educator. I assisted him when he was the middle school basketball coach. What would make this different? It wouldn't be different. I would see it as helping him to carry on God's work. Then I realized something. This would be a major turning point in my understanding of my new role. I would be helping him to carry on God's work, something I already enjoyed doing. That's it!

I wondered why I didn't receive "the call" just as he had. But I was mistaken. My call wasn't new. I had a calling on my life from early on, to love God and His people just as He loves me. I was looking for something dramatic to happen. My calling was not one to change, it was one to expand what I was already doing. I did not understand it during His revelation period. While these "questions" were floating in my mind, my heavenly Father heard them and began to answer them. I just needed to listen for his response. As a result of my ear tuning into different sources, it would take me longer to hear exactly what God was saying to me.

ALL THE PREACHER'S WIVES
A Peek Behind The Curtain Of Being A Preacher's Wife

How was I supposed to support my husband's ministry when the actions I saw outside of the church did not align with my idea of a preacher? I know many of you may be thinking, "what kind of actions?" I know you do not have to be perfect to be utilized in God's ministry. Nevertheless, what I saw was far from being considered perfect. I was not judging him because I was taught against assigning judgment to a person. What I visualized, heard, and endured was as far from the ministry as the east is from the west. This is where my confusion originated. Yet, I was still trying to figure things out on my own.

He accepted his calling. Immediately this turned into multiple church visits with him desiring to sit in the pulpit with the other ministers. We attended two different church services in one day (sometimes three) to become known in the ministry. I enjoyed seeing the different orders of worship and learning about the beliefs of the different denominations, yet it did not afford me the chance to get to really know anyone at the churches. I became a regular visitor, not having membership in either church. This was confusing at the time. Through all of this, what I didn't realize was that God was preparing me for the ministry to come. Eventually, my husband would pastor three churches simultaneously and I would need to become immersed in all three congregations for our ministry to be effective. This task would challenge me. It was eleven years earlier that God had begun my training and preparation. He was speaking and I couldn't hear Him.

Then my husband began to become relaxed with not working. He only studied his scriptures and played golf, which was his way of relaxing. All of the financial responsibilities were placed upon me. I saw it as unfair, especially when I was in school myself, pursuing a degree that would allow me to keep my job as an educator, and helping him to critique and edit his writings. I could not understand how he had so much "free time" while I was struggling to get in bed before 1 a.m. I dare not ask him to assist me in my work, or even the cleaning around the apartment or parsonage. He would always be too busy or too tired to help. I felt God disliked me, but little did I know He was preparing me for when I would have to work a demanding job, write, teach his

ALL THE PREACHER'S WIVES
A Peek Behind The Curtain Of Being A Preacher's Wife

Bible studies week after week, and write or edit his papers while he worked on an advanced degree for the ministry. I did not have the vision to know that one day all that energy would be poured into my own business, writing, publishing, photography, and being an advocate for others. Little did I know, but I would later find out. I still wasn't listening.

Once he preached his first sermon, this was it. Now he could be recognized as a reverend. Maybe life would be easier now. He didn't have to work so hard to prove he had accepted his calling. It was now part of his title, Reverend. That was it. It was a part of his identity. However, he began to think the title made him *entitled*. His expectations rose while his responsibilities diminished. I was delegated to being like an usher in our home. I was summoned to bring him things, like a glass of water, something to eat, or a book he needed for reference. None of this would have bothered me if it had been a mutual action. There were times when I needed things because I was in the middle of working on something and he couldn't step away from what he was doing. Then when I did get up, I found his eyes glued to the television watching a sporting event. Several times I had the feeling of being used. It was during these times that God was preparing me for service to His people. As the first lady of one of our churches, I would often have to remove my heels and stand in as an usher to welcome people as they entered our sanctuary. This was a task better suited for the younger, more able-bodied people. He was still speaking, and I couldn't hear Him.

Then there were the expectations he had of me. He expected me to dress provocatively when in his presence, not just at home, but at church also. My skirts could not be too long, my pantsuits could not be too loose. I must have on make-up, including lashes, and high-heeled shoes. This was a requirement because he wanted others to see me as desirable, thus increasing his value because he was able to snag *me* as a wife. This made me feel quite uncomfortable because if others spoke a little nicer to me than they did to others, or looked in my direction too intently, he would accuse me of being flirtatious or desiring the man. I became terrified to even speak with another man, no matter who it was. If he saw me talk to them, or heard that I was talking to them, he would require me to report the entire conversation verbatim. This became such an arduous task that I just began to avoid every male I saw. It didn't matter who it was, a friend, family member, or a stranger. If I could not repeat every word said, I was hiding something. It almost sent me back to my recluse stage. As a diagnosed severe manic depressive (now referred to as Bipolar 2 disorder), I was comfortable being secluded from everyone. I had low self-esteem and feared each time I had to be in a situation with a male because I did not want to have to explain the encounter. So, I always kept to myself, not opening myself up to discussions unless I was in his presence. Soon this turned into him always being in my presence. At first, I thought it was him desiring to be with me. Later I found out he just didn't want anyone else to want to be with me. How could God allow me to be in so much hell? I did not realize at the time that He was preparing me to know how to be in public situations but stay out of trouble's way; how to keep confidential things to myself and to avoid situations that would put me in compromising positions. He spoke, but I was not listening.

    On top of all this, there were his multiple encounters with women. He would be extremely friendly with women in my presence but dare me to ask him anything about the conversation or relationship. Wait, wasn't this a double standard? Yes, it was. Nevertheless, I knew better than to inquire. The friendliness turned into time spent talking with them, counseling them, and advising them, all of which required him to be confidential, but the inappropriate times of the interaction did not align with ministerial duties. I did understand that the ministry of a preacher/pastor did not always adhere to office hours, but I also understood that hours of jovial talking on the phone and requests for him to make them comfortable did not always refer to a God-led event. I could not hear God's voice trying to tell me that this was preparing me for the mistreatment I would sometimes receive from parishioners who envied my position as the pastor's wife. The dirty looks came. Sometimes blatant negative comments without cause or reason were

ALL THE PREACHER'S WIVES
A Peek Behind The Curtain Of Being A Preacher's Wife

the reaction I got from some women. He spoke in a whisper, but I was listening for a loud cry.

I wasn't good enough. I had begun to think that this lifelong mantra I repeated to myself was true. Yes, the first lady who was treated as a trophy wife in public was not good enough. Where did I get this thought from? It wasn't the many parishioners who supported me week by week with kind words and concerns. It wasn't my family who I was rarely allowed to communicate with. It wasn't even my "haters" who wanted to be in what they perceived my position to be. I didn't listen to them because of their unimportance. It was him, the closest person to me (or who was supposed to be). He told me several times that he had opportunities to be with others if he wanted to. Once, after he asked my opinion of a discussion at a Bible study, and I disagreed with what he said, he left me at the church (but we were in separate cars, he just always used to follow me home), and kept me locked out of the bedroom for three days. I could not get ready for work until he left home. My response was according to the Word of God, not emotional feelings of disrespect. I could not acknowledge that being disrespected allowed you to disregard what the Word said. I could not understand how he could justify it either, not as a pastor. So, on the morning after my second day on lock-out, he proceeded to tell me, "I have plenty of prospects to be the next Mrs. _____. I *hope* you can find someone who wants you." Those twenty words sent me on a downward spiral I thought I could never get out of. It solidified my diminished value, at least to me. What I didn't realize was He was preparing me to be able to relate to the downtrodden and mistreated on a personal level. He was preparing me for my second phase of ministry. He spoke to me, but it fell on deaf ears.

None of this was enough to make me leave. I thought I was doing the right thing by staying. I was from the time when divorce was not seen favorably in the church, especially when it was leaving the pastor. If he is a man of God, it must be something wrong with me for leaving. Plus, his father had told me that my leaving would cause the church to split. There I was, stuck to live this life of turmoil as service to the master. Well, I was partially correct. It was servicing the master, but I did not understand who I actually was servicing. I listened to the wrong source for my direction. I drowned out the voice of God and listened to the pastor's voice because it was louder and more forceful. Besides, if God "called" him, then it had to be my role to listen to him and adhere. Therefore, I tried to cultivate the marriage relationship. I kept quiet about the mistreatment at home. I kept quiet when he spat on me, cursed me, and threatened to kill me. I continued to submit to him because I saw it as part of God's Word. That is where I was wrong. I only focused on Ephesians 5:22-23. The importance of what I missed is outlined in Ephesians 5:25-30. The husbands should love their wives as God loves the church. The level of mistreatment I endured was not part of the scripture. It was not a component of ministry, not God's ministry.

I had been cultivating the wrong relationship. I made my husband (now ex-husband) the master. I served him the best way I knew how. I bent over backwards, made sacrifices (like eating one bowl of cereal a day so he could have money to buy clothes in order to look the part), and took the verbal and financial abuse from him as my duty to the church. All along, I prayed for God to change him. If God "called" him, it must be something about him that is beneficial to God's ministry. As I waited to see his "change" coming, I continued to engross myself in servicing the congregation and community. I tutored children who needed assistance (no pay involved until he saw it as an income opportunity). I learned and taught new songs to the choir. I wrote and taught Bible study so well that sometimes the pastor would come to just listen. I visited and talked with the elderly who just wanted to know someone cared. I offered my assistance to anyone who could utilize it. I was ministering to the people, not from behind the pulpit, but in front of it, where they needed it.

What did this do for the marriage? It created a very rocky relationship between my husband and myself because I began to see value in myself. At 41, I became pregnant for the first time. This, I felt, was God making things right for me. If my husband wouldn't treat me like he loved me, well, this baby would. However, due to the negativity he always carried in his heart toward me, he argued with me about nothing every night. I didn't understand it, but I felt that saying something would help me to defend myself. Church members began to reach out saying things like, "we are here for you," and "we can see what is going on." God was trying to intervene, but I was taking matters into my own hands. This led me to two miscarriages within 6 months. That was it. It was confirmed in my mind that I was not good enough. I was not a good enough wife because I couldn't keep my husband happy. I was not a good enough first lady because I had allowed the parishioners to see a glimpse of my home life (unbeknownst to me). I was not a good enough Christian because God did not see fit for me to be a mother. I stopped listening completely. The noise now overshadowed my hearing. I was lost.

Interestingly enough, this is when things began to get crystal clear. I had my relationship with my husband trying to overshadow my relationship with God. I vowed to please him instead of pleasing Him. The Bible clearly states that we are not to have two masters (Matt. 6:24), and I was in clear violation. All this time, for years, I had pleaded with God to change him, make him into whom I envisioned him to be. All the while God was speaking to me, telling me to change. I was flawed. My ministry for Him could only go so far because I was cultivating the wrong relationship. I had to pray and listen for God's voice to give me direction. He didn't speak loudly, but He spoke consistently. It was up to me to hear Him. So, I began to take notice of how good it felt to go the extra mile to provide service where needed. I relinquished my place at the head of the food line in church (the pastor and the first lady always were fed first) and instead began serving the elderly who needed assistance to get around. I started spending more time with my family, even when he did not approve because my relationship with them provided peace, while his provided turmoil. God was making the necessary changes in me that allowed me more time to work in His vineyard.

ALL THE PREACHER'S WIVES
A Peek Behind The Curtain Of Being A Preacher's Wife

I continued to stay and work within the church and community until our marriage dissolved. Because of the abrupt way I had to leave, I was sure it would create some type of damage within the church. To my surprise, it didn't! They continued to go to church and support the ministry, and they reached out to me to let me know that I am always welcome there. The things I did there were immensely helpful to our small congregations. Whether it was helping them with paperwork, tutoring kids and grandkids, or helping in food/clothes donations, it was all appreciated and welcomed. Even though I was estranged from my husband, I did not become estranged from ministry. Instead, just the opposite happened.

My ministry became more than just the people in our church community. Once I divorced, I was now able to minister to those in rocky marriages, trying to show them how important communication is and how detrimental failed communication could be. Because I now knew what it was like to have your spouse pull a firearm on you, I could speak to those victims of domestic abuse and let them know there is life after divorce or separation. Because I came close to losing my life to suicide, I could now minister to those whose thoughts of ending their lives are real. Because I have a God who taught us how to forgive, I could minister to those who found it difficult to forgive their abuser. My ministry had never ended. The entire time I was fine-tuning the ministry that was to come.

After losing my cousin to domestic violence (I had already lost an aunt and a classmate that way), I made a promise to God that if He would provide the opportunity, I would use my voice to speak for those who couldn't speak for themselves. This included more than just domestic abuse victims, but also those suffering from mental health issues and social injustice. Now I get to do just that. I am an author and poetess who uses my words to make a difference in someone's life. I write thought-provoking pieces to get others to see things in ways they haven't been required before. I own Busta Word Publishing, LLC which gives writers a chance to let their voices be heard. I partner with my local domestic abuse shelter to provide donations and bring

ALL THE PREACHER'S WIVES
A Peek Behind The Curtain Of Being A Preacher's Wife

awareness to their cause. I have even spoken to share my story on their behalf. All this time, through all this pain, God was preparing me for greater. My goal was to see a change in the pastor. His goal was to see a change in me. His goals were realized and today, I am known publicly as "The Voice," a moniker not given to me by myself, but assigned to me through divine intervention from God through my poet friends. God reminded me of my promise. He continues to remind me of my mission. I am elated that He no longer has to remind me who is the Master. Our relationship is now better than ever. I thank God that He didn't give up on me. I'm still listening.

To any spouse reading this wondering if this is normal activity for the pastoral ministry, it is not. Nothing is normal because it is all relative to the situation you are in. You can expect the ministry to be trying at times because it becomes an integral part of your relationship. Nevertheless, it should never replace your relationship with God or your spouse. It should serve as an enhancement. Do not allow issues to build up for the sake of saving face. Talk about it within your home. Don't be afraid to speak to a licensed counselor, if needed. The ministry is filled with taking on or listening to the trials and tribulations of others. This can be challenging if you are already having issues with the two of you. Nonetheless, never allow your own value to be diminished to make others feel good about themselves. Seek help. Turn to God. But most importantly, listen when He speaks.

Co-Pastor Brandie Manigault

"Even in the whispers and secret discussions, they gave us our space but made it clear – they didn't want anything to do with what we were doing."

ALL THE PREACHER'S WIVES
A Peek Behind The Curtain Of Being A Preacher's Wife

5
The Fear In Love

My story is one riddled with the highest of highs, the lowest of lows, and everything in between. It is one of ranging from knowing whom I am to not having a clue, and then going on a journey to rediscover myself all over again. It is about me doing the work to become someone that I am proud of; someone that I love; someone that I would be ok with if my girls decided to be like me.

I have been married for over a decade and a half and in that time, I have moved from the east coast to the west coast, from the west coast to the middle of the country, back to the west and now am currently settled in the middle again. I have four beautiful children whom I have given my whole life to make sure that they know that they are loved and supported. When my husband and I got married, he said I didn't have to work again if I didn't want to. Having had some kind of job since I was 14 years old, that offer was appealing, and I took him up on it. I wanted to be home. I wanted to build a home. I wanted to make sure that I was available for every game my kids had, every play date they wanted to go on, every parent-teacher conference, and every event they had at school. I wanted to give them what my parents gave me. One of the things that I will always be able to say about my childhood is that my parents loved me and supported me. In middle school, I played in the band and played softball and basketball. Then I went on to play basketball and run track in high school. What I

ALL THE PREACHER'S WIVES
A Peek Behind The Curtain Of Being A Preacher's Wife

remember about those years was that my parents were at every concert, game, and meet. The only games I remember my dad missing was when he was deployed somewhere, but that didn't stop my mom from coming to cheer us on. That is the memory that I wanted my kids to talk about when they are adults. Undoubtedly, there are many things that I have gotten wrong over the years, but "showing up" isn't one of them.

I'm pretty sure that a good part of the time I was unhealthily and unevenly balancing my devotion to the kids with me being a stay home wife and with my own dreams and aspirations. I rationalized it by saying, "they need me. He can wait. I can wait." A mistake in judgment that has taken me many years to course correct, and still falls back into the familiar trap of putting them front and center of my world, forsaking all else. I'm forever a work in progress!

Over the course of our marriage and time in ministries, we have been afforded opportunities to travel the world, see the most beautiful of places, meet the most amazing individuals, and serve ministries and organizations that people could only dream of. My husband and I have hosted worship conferences, healing conferences, young leaders' conferences, and worship nights seeing God move in both power and in silent moments. God has allowed me to do life with people who have loved me and loved me well.

On the flip side of that same coin has been heartache and heartbreak, betrayal, pain like I had never known, depression, and darkness. I sacrificed myself on the altar of ministry time and time again. It sounds good to say that our job is to always be there for people, always meet needs, look at the greater good and do whatever needs to be done to make sure God's people are taken care of, but we do it... I did it at my own expense time and time again. I looked at the impact and fruit of my husband's time and investment in other people's lives and said it was worth the late nights, the long meetings, the time he spent pouring into them, and the endless resources we made available to them. I resented my sacrifices even and at the same time relished being able to help.

I say that I sacrificed myself because as a result of my constant "giving," my needs continued to go unmet. I always allowed someone else's needs to be the priority. What it came down to was that I value others more than I valued myself. I didn't think that I was worthy of the same investment. Someone else's pain was always more pronounced and more pressing than my own.

I learned to live with feeling unseen and unattended in that way; like I didn't need to be ministered to. I learned to not express what I needed because when you are constantly let down by unmet expectations you learn to not express them at all. It minimizes disappointment. You can tell yourself that they didn't do it because they didn't know when the reality is that I should have been my own advocate and I wasn't. Lesson learned though!

Thinking back, I never really wanted to be a pastor's wife. I just wanted to be a "normal" Christian who went to church and went home. I thought that I would just pick a church, one with great praise and worship, a dynamic preacher, one not too big but not too small. I wanted to blend in but be noticed at the same time if I missed a service. I thought I might volunteer to be a greeter on an occasional Sunday if it didn't interfere with watching the Raven's football game. I just wanted to go to church and go home.

The funny thing is that as a teenager, my friend and I always said we were going to have a church together. We lived about an hour away from each other so we decided that it would be halfway between our two cities, and that put us in Kenosha, WI. I had only been there a handful of times, but it worked out for us both on the map, so Kenosha it was! As we grew up that co-lead dream faded into the background of college, relocations, and life.

ALL THE PREACHER'S WIVES
A Peek Behind The Curtain Of Being A Preacher's Wife

Seeing even a small portion behind the scenes of any organization has the potential to change how you see working with that organization. Church and ministry were no exception. I had seen behind the curtain just enough to not want to deal with the politics or demands of church leadership at that point in time. I decided that I didn't want to give my whole life to being at the beck and call of people for the rest of my life.

It's interesting how when you meet a man and fall in love, you reconsider things that you had once given a hard "no" to. I remember having a conversation with my then-boyfriend and him saying, "I'm going to be a pastor one day. Are you good with that?". Of course, I was. I loved him. I also didn't think he was serious! He was a singer. I thought that would be his contribution to the church…not as a pastor.

Fast forward a few years, and he gets offered a position as a worship pastor for a church in Southern California. By now we knew that we were going to get married. It was just a matter of when. I often joke and say, "we were too broke to get married". It was much cheaper to live at my parents' house with one singular bill other than my highly discounted rental rate. My then-boyfriend moved down to Baltimore from the Bronx to be closer to me. He worked two jobs and rented out my parents' basement, but even with his discounted rent and mine combined, it was still cheaper than us having a place of our own with all the expenses that being married came with. So, we waited. We waited three years. To be fair, a year and a half of that were him finishing college. We both went to Oral Roberts University in Tulsa, OK. I graduated in May of 2003 and he in 2004. So, there was the time to finish school combined with the time to get employed and be able to sustain a family.

With this new job offer pending, it would require him to relocate to the other side of the country. The realization of a long-distance relationship was quite sobering. Neither of us wanted that, and with this new salary, we could "afford" to get married and start our life together. Now was the time. We got engaged in November, got married on a Saturday in March, and that Sunday we relocated from Maryland to California.

To say I was culture shocked is an understatement. To say I didn't feel like I fit in is an even bigger understatement. The people were different. It felt like the values were different. I'm from Baltimore so sometimes my speech betrays me! Baltimoreans have a way of leaving out crucial letters in words when speaking, and there is a way that certain words are pronounced that will absolutely have people asking, "Where are you from?". I didn't mind it. Still don't, but at the time we were newlyweds, just starting out with this new church, in a new location, and the last thing I wanted to do was embarrass my husband or say something that would get him fired. I did say we were newlyweds. Employment was important!

In everyday conversation at home, my husband would joke about how I said certain words. "Babe. It's hot DOG, not hot DUG". The more comfortable I am the more relaxed I am in general, and at home, I am quite relaxed, less guarded, and less intentional about how I pronounce things.

It was the little jokes and corrections that, in a normal context wouldn't mean anything, but to a woman battling with her own insecurities, it was a big deal. And of course, I didn't tell him that's how I felt. Why would I be vulnerable with my husband? Why would I tell him that I felt like he was trying to change me or that I felt like he was trying to be someone he was not around these new people? Why would I set myself up to be misunderstood and rejected? (Written with a lot of sarcasm!)

It wasn't just the way I said things though. It was also what I said. I was so full of fear that I started practicing the art of silence. I was invited into rooms and spaces with him with other pastors and leaders and would be asked my opinion on different subjects, but the

ALL THE PREACHER'S WIVES
A Peek Behind The Curtain Of Being A Preacher's Wife

fear of saying the wrong thing kept me from saying much. I had an opinion. I had thoughts. I wanted to voice them. I did not want to be judged by them. I didn't want anyone to think I wasn't good enough to be in that space anymore. I didn't want them to judge my husband based on his wife's thoughts and opinions.

So, after practicing silence for so long and mastering it, I started just declining invitations to the rooms I desperately wanted to be in with him. It was easier to reject myself than to be rejected by others. My husband expressed his desire for me to be there. He told me how much he wanted me around, but I felt like it was an obligatory invitation because other wives were there, or he just wanted to make me feel good.

It wasn't until many years later that I realize that he actually meant it. He really did want me there. He wasn't trying to change me or make me be a certain way. He did feel the pressure of constantly being "on" and not jeopardizing his job, but he didn't realize that at the same time that he was feeling the pressure that I was feeling as well.

What I find ironic is that before we got married, we talked all the time, for hours on end and about everything, but when we got married, we stopped talking about the important things, the major life changes we had embarked on together, or the impact of joining our two lives together. We slid into roles that nurtured job security and public image, but not so much our home life. We were happy. We had fun together. We traveled and experienced new things together. But we didn't learn how to communicate our new wants and needs as a married couple. It was easy when we were dating. We dreamed of a life together, but when we got it I don't think either one of us really understood what was needed to live the dream out.

About two years into being married, my mother told me "Don't lose yourself in being Tim's wife". It was the best advice that I ever abided by. By the time she told me these great words of wisdom it was already too late. She saw something that I had gradually succumbed to, and because it was such a gradual change, I didn't see it. People would introduce me as "Pastor Tim's wife". I didn't have a name. I became so used to being nameless that when I had children, I became the children's mother, and I wore it like a badge of honor. I'd walk on campus at the kids' school and both the kids and teachers alike would wave saying, "hi Sydney's mom" or whichever kid they identified with. I was ok with being unseen. Being unseen actually became so familiar that it felt safe and comfortable. I knew what to expect behind the scenes

I also realized many years and therapy dollars later that hiding in the shadows was my way of relinquishing my responsibilities. I could pass the blame to someone else if I wasn't the decision-maker. I deferred to my husband a lot for "approval" so that he would be held responsible if it didn't work out… whatever the "it" was. What therapy taught me was that my silence and inaction were still an action that I had to take responsibility for. I chose to not say anything. I chose not to have input. I chose to allow things to happen the way they did. No one can be held accountable for that but me; just like I am not responsible for other people's choices, no one is responsible for mine. It's actually been quite freeing to live into that realization. I can own my life and my words.

I know therapy is hit or miss in the church world, but I am still married and living a wonderful life because I made the decision to go to a licensed professional for help. Twelve years into our marriage, trauma pushed us into a place where we had to make the decision to fight for ourselves or walk away from ourselves. We were at our absolute lowest and needed all of the help that we could get if we would have any hope of surviving. So, we started couples therapy, and it was the best decision we could have ever made. It saved our marriage. It gave us the tools that we needed to communicate and work through twelve years of misunderstanding, miscommunication, hurt, and pain. It helped us identify both the truths and the lies that we had been living

ALL THE PREACHER'S WIVES
A Peek Behind The Curtain Of Being A Preacher's Wife

with for all those years. Therapy helped me to see him again and him to see me. Somewhere in our journey together we lost ourselves. We no longer saw our best friend. Life happened. Children happened. Work happened. Ministry happened. Schedules happened. All the things happened, and we did not intentionally keep ourselves as the main thing. We took for granted that we would always be there. It was true. No matter what happened at the end of the day it was us. Some days felt more like roommates than lovers, single parenting versus parenting,

There was a time when I actually thought to myself, I could do this without him, and the only thing that kept me from completely disconnecting was the thought that "my son needed his father in the house". I'm not sure why I didn't have that same thought about my girls needing him to be present. The truth was the same, they needed him as much as my son did, but there was something about a boy and his dad that felt like a layer of protection and raising that I couldn't give him. The idea of my son having him as an everyday presence did something to me, and that is what I held onto until we got help.

Reaching out to my therapist for the very first time changed the trajectory of where my life was heading. It is the gift that continues to give even to this day. Therapy gave me my voice back. I wasn't aware of the depth of silence I was operating in until one day I went to pray, and no words came out of my mouth. It wasn't new, I had just noticed it. Raising four children you get consumed with that world. There aren't many adults to talk to as a stay-at-home mom. When the children are in school, the house is empty and there is no one to exchange words with on a regular, consistent basis. Most of my days were spent in the quiet. So, when I would pray, I also prayed in silence. I mostly talked to the Lord in my head. It went on like that for years.

I got used to not hearing my own voice. Then one day I started talking in a mom group and I felt empowered. I felt strong. I felt like I had something to say and to people who would "get it"; who would get me. I was still relatively quiet in other circles, but with this group, I felt like I had something to contribute. I stayed with that group for a little over two years, gaining my confidence back with each week that passed.

It was all lost again, having to be rebuilt after a series of traumatic experiences struck my marriage, my family, our church, and our community. Silence became my friend and comforter again.

Enter my therapist. Weekly sessions for a year. Biweekly for another year. Once a month for six months. Periodic check-ins.

The other side of the pain feels so good!
The other side of healing is freedom!
The community was built, lost, and built again.

There is a piece of me that died at the onset of trauma that was reborn in a 2.0, upgraded edition. It was as if everything that prohibited me from being me was burned in a fire and all that was left was this bolder and more confident version of the person I learned how to be.

There are days even now that I look at myself in the mirror and wonder whom that girl was that used to stare back at me. How did I let it get that far? Then gratefulness kicks in and all I can do is thank God that I didn't let the pain create a version of me that I hated.

Out of the place of pain was birthed freedom to live unapologetically, to fight for what I believe in, to speak for my convictions, to not be ashamed to stand with both the victim and the violator, and to love people right where they are- in their mess or at the highest moments. After years of counseling and meetings with a team focused solely on our health and restoration, we returned back to the ministry, but this time as lead pastors.

ALL THE PREACHER'S WIVES
A Peek Behind The Curtain Of Being A Preacher's Wife

My husband was always a pastor on staff in the different churches that he worked for, but this time he asked me if I felt called to pastor with him. Deep inside I knew the answer was yes, but there was great hesitation to accept it. I had seen the toll it takes. I had seen the sacrifice it required and that was made even when not required. Could my marriage handle it again? Could I handle the pressure? Could I do it? Would people respect me in that space? Did I have anything to offer?

I gave him a no out of fear.

Enter a prophet in Tulsa with no knowledge of anything I had been contemplating or the no I had just given. She then, in no uncertain terms, told me it was time to say yes! We left the venue and my husband looked at me and laughed.

When we started Ecos Church we were in a building doing the normal church things. We had a worship team, announcements, giving, the message, altar calls, fellowships time, etc. When the pandemic hit, we shifted our in-person church to online with the rest of the world. What we didn't know at the time was that the Lord's plan for us was and still is for us to remain online while the rest of the world returns to its buildings.

We went from a few families on a Sunday and a monthly community night of worship in Southern California to the majority of the Ecos Everywhere family being on the east coast. As an online church, we are intentional about having local footprints by partnering with churches and outreaches across the country. We have had to really learn the voice of God in a new way for this new way of doing church. Small groups look different. The community looks different. Services look different. Our mandate is "to build the family of God around the presence of God." The building looks different. One thing for sure is that He gives you the grace to do what He asks you to do and to pivot when He says pivot.

ALL THE PREACHER'S WIVES
A Peek Behind The Curtain Of Being A Preacher's Wife

When the Lord said for us to stay online, we didn't know that He was going to shift us from California to Texas. We weren't aware of His big-picture plan for our family at the time but looking back it makes so much sense. If we had stuck to the building because it's "how the church is supposed to be done", we wouldn't have been able to relocate with the freedom to still minister to "hearts and homes" like He said for us to do.

He wanted our "yes" at each phase without us knowing what the big picture looked like.

We moved to Texas because He said it was time. My family is healthy and thriving here because we told him "Yes" as a family; all six of us gave Him a "yes", and we took the leap of faith together.

ALL THE PREACHER'S WIVES
A Peek Behind The Curtain Of Being A Preacher's Wife

Dr. Trivia Payne

"I had just started a nasty divorce process and I knew that when I graduated from college my daughters and I were going to move to Virginia to start a new life."

6
To Be or Not to Be a Preacher's Wife

For the bulk of my life, I attended churches where the Pastor was a woman. After having my second child at the age of twenty, I heard a term for the first time. I never paid it any mind, but I knew that this was an important role in the church. This term, unbeknownst to me, can be used in different ways across various denominations in leadership and in the church. These terms were "The Preacher's wife", "The First Lady", "The Leading Lady", and "The Pastor's wife".

My first experience with a "First Lady" was this amazing lady who was classy, very quiet and never needed an introduction because she had a voice that always took me back to my apostolic church days. Lady Hannah was her name and she made being a "First Lady" look easy. My next experience with a "First Lady" was when I was working at a church in a leadership position, and she was never formally introduced until I had a little too many meetings with the Pastor. I wasn't a member of the church by the way. I was approached and called into a meeting with her. My view of a Pastor's wife changed drastically. I didn't understand why she was overreacting.

The irony of that situation was that it was taking place during a time when I was reconnecting with a high school friend after fourteen years. While engaging in the situation with the second "First Lady," the

ALL THE PREACHER'S WIVES
A Peek Behind The Curtain Of Being A Preacher's Wife

term "First Lady" was still foreign to me. Women who had previously held these positions had always been addressed as Pastor So-and-So's wife for example. I never understood why the pastor required overprotecting from his staff members or his wife in general. Yet, in reconnecting with my high school friend, I recall saying to him after a few months of talking on the phone purely out of nowhere that I am called to be a "First Lady".

My friend never said anything about my statement outside of "Really?" I explained that I didn't know what a "First Lady" was or even what she did. We continued talking for almost a year and continued studying the Bible as we had done since we reconnected.

My friend never once told me what kind of work he did, but I was informed that he was very instrumental in his church at the time and in his previous church. The funny thing is after meeting in high school, my mother took me to a church where he was a member, and we began going to church together. I knew he was a believer, and I knew him to be a very compassionate young guy. The challenge of it all was at the time of this reconnection, he was incarcerated serving a lengthy sentence.

It wasn't until we reconnected that things began to change in both of our lives. I was a mother of five young daughters, preparing to graduate from college after 12 years of trying to get my life together. I had just started a nasty divorce process and I knew that when I graduated from college my daughters and I were going to move to Virginia to start a new life. For my Friend, he had just transferred to the city and was waiting on the process of an early release. I remember it like yesterday. We were having conversations as we always did, but we started talking about what God says about divorce. Within two months of my ex trying to take my girls from me, the judge granted us a divorce. That was November 21st, 2007, after being legally married for 10 years.

By 2008, as I walked into the building of my friend's graduation, I had no idea that at the end, I would be walking out an engaged woman. I still had no idea when I made the statement of being a "First Lady," that God was already planning out the details. In August of 2008 when my fiancé walked free from the system, our lives began to change again. He immediately started a ministry which was something he had planned to do for years prior to coming home from incarceration, and my view of those incarcerated changed so that it lined up with the will of my husband-to-be.

A woman who once feared men of the streets was now doing ministry with men returning to society from incarceration. Within a year of his release, we were married, and shortly after, I became the wife of an ordained elder. Did I mention, while engaged, and after the release of my fiancé at the time, we spent endless hours discussing what it looks like for our family once we were married, and he became a pastor? When you don't come from a background of ministry, you must base your morals and expectations on your life experiences.

We discussed the idea that many pastors would devote more time to the ministry and neglect family. In our mind that would not be us. We also discussed how being in private places with or visiting the opposite sex would be something that we would never do. That was something we both agreed on. Looking back in hindsight, that needed a deeper conversation. There were so many conversations that we had prior to marriage and ministry, and I was getting excited. I was going to be there to support whatever my husband, now pastor, believed God had in store for us. My husband was to be the king of our castle and the pastor of our families. I trusted God in his life even though we had challenges. I soon realized that being that supportive, dedicated wife was not going to be an immediate undertaking.

I can recall the night like it was yesterday. We were married for about two months, and we had just finished an evening of strong disagreement. As usual, I would get far away from him, and he would go directly to the Word or pray. I was in my room and heard him calling me with a sense of urgency. When I got to the living room where he was, it was like we weren't in a bad place. His words to me were "I heard from God, and He is saying that this is going to be our first home for men coming home from prison." As usual, I didn't ask any questions. I responded with, "If God said it, then alright." I think that day made it simple for my husband to come to me and say what God said and I never disregarded the God in him. Within six months, we opened our transitional house the same day we moved into our new house. Not long after, we began having weekly Bible studies and then moved into having bi-weekly Sunday worship services for men coming home from incarceration and their families.

Things were going well for my family and me in ministry, or so I thought. We had a ministry for men coming home from prison, we had a bi-weekly Sunday worship service, and started a house where men could come home and not worry about bills or the stressors of life. After a few months had passed, we decided to start a full-time church. We were no longer visiting other churches twice a month, the responsibility of full-time pastoring became our reality. The only problem was that I instantly became a pastor's wife, and our children became PK's (Preacher Kids). That vision that I received years earlier was coming to pass. I was going into a crisis.

Greatest Challenge as a Preacher's wife:

I began having a sense of lost identity. I was living in the shadow of my husband. My name became Pastor Antoine's wife. My pastor-husband was receiving all the accolades for the transition happening in our lives. Our girls and I were in the background being his cheerleaders. Wherever he went, we were there. I was his armor-bearer, and our girls were the hype men. They danced before he preached. We went around with him faithfully, but while the church was developing and forming, our family was quickly fading away and I felt that we were being overshadowed by the new cheerleaders.

As membership grew, we shifted from just a ministry of men coming home to the addition of other female cheerleaders. My husband and I really grew apart. In my mind, I was attacked by the church members and my husband didn't know how to protect me from the congregation. I felt that low one time before. By this time, though I supported my pastor-husband, it was under the premise that this was the kind of life that I walked into. Apparently, God wanted me to deal with this kind of hurt. This was my reality. Otherwise, why would God

ALL THE PREACHER'S WIVES
A Peek Behind The Curtain Of Being A Preacher's Wife

allow me to marry him? I began to feel pained spiritually, mentally, and moreover physically.

Spiritually. I did everything except become angry with God. I was being beaten with the Bible. I would cry because my attention span was so low, and I thought that I had to pray for hours and hours because everyone else did. I was a worker and server and the people who I now fellowshipped with were showing me up because they had no problem meeting the requirements of the pastor. I thought that because I was struggling to be like the other members of the church, I wasn't where God wanted me to be. Although I had obtained a college degree, I hated reading. I would get sick to my stomach and would cry because we would have to stand up and read whole chapters in the Bible to the group, and to me that was a bit much. In my mind, we weren't meeting members where they were. In my mind, I was on a spiritual decline. Little did I know, God was raising me for something even greater.

Mentally. I was breaking by the day. I walked around fighting my feelings because whenever I would respond to my feelings, my lashing out was huge. I was taking lashings from the members, my pastor-husband, and then lashings from myself. I thought about all of the ways in which I could harm myself and the only thing that kept me was knowing that should I harm myself, I had five beautiful daughters that needed me. My self-esteem was low, and I could care less about self-care which gave the strong-willed members weapons to use against me. I battled depression, and at the same time, I wanted to break generational curses. When I became a pastor's wife, it seemed as if I was hitting walls of emotional whirlwinds.

Physically. No one understood the pain that I was feeling. I became very angry. I placed the fact that sexually I couldn't satisfy my husband and thought that it was from the sexual misconduct from my past, only to learn that I was in so much pain because I was dealing with "an issue of blood." Physically everything was connecting, and I was unintentionally allowing my pain to build walls between my pastor-husband and me. What I failed to realize at the time was before we could connect, though eventually we did, my strength and growth regarding my marriage had to be in alignment.

I was spiritually disconnected from God. I didn't realize that the physical pain in my body was causing me to turn away from God and anyone else willing to help. My mental state was impacted even more because of my physical pain and disconnect from God. I didn't have enough wisdom to share where I was with those who loved and cared for me. As a new pastor's wife, I had to realize that I would be just as much under a microscope as my husband. The only difference was that I wasn't receiving a stipend for it.

Finding support

At this point, I was connecting to other pastors' wives' whose husbands were connected to my husband-pastor. Initially trying to build connections with the wives was not what I imagined. At first, I was very introverted. I didn't want anyone to touch, nonetheless, hug me. The feeling was mutual. I would reach out at the most pivotal times in my marriage and ministry, but I couldn't seem to find one pastor's wife who would mentor me, much less be my friend. My husband and I were young in ministry and young period. But whenever he walked into a room, especially full of those who knew of his background, his presence demanded respect without him opening his mouth. (Probably because he looked like a linebacker. Just kidding.) But when I walked into a room, I felt like a little ant that everyone wanted to avoid. The interesting thing was I grew out of ant status and started being identified as the Pastor's wife.

I was at my lowest point in ministry and living in the shadow of my husband. I didn't know what was expected of me, nor did I know how to navigate the things that I believed God's will was for my life. I got to a point in ministry where I didn't want to have any part to do with ministry or the people connected to the ministry. I felt like I was in a world of my own. When I tried to gain an understanding from women who were already pastor wives, I found that they could not help

me because they had their own challenges. In hindsight, the ones who had been in ministry longer were probably reluctant to connect with me because they had already dealt with the growing pains of marriage and ministry. My breakdowns occurred daily. I cried out to God asking whom I could connect to that would understand what I was going through. I received a call one day that went a little something like this
Caller: Hello, how are you Lady Trivia
Me: How are you, Auntie?
Caller: We are starting a First Ladies' Club and I wanted to know if this is something that you would be interested in.
Me: (Tears began to fall). Of course.
I explained that I was tapped out and had just prayed about this.

    I didn't know what to expect, but I knew that it was the immediate answer to a long cry to the Father. As I sat on the side of my bed, I was so overwhelmed by how much God loves me so. He didn't let me break, but He let me know that when I had no one else to depend on, I could depend on Him, He was right there in the midst. Within a month of that call, we held our first pastor's wife's club meeting.

    When I say that God is on time, He is truly on time. To sit in the room with pastors' wives who were both seasoned and new to the calling, I realized that I wasn't the only pastor's wife experiencing a difficult season. There were women of God who were able to stand in the gap and intercede on behalf of marriages and ministries knowing that being a pastor's wife was not only a calling but also a gift from God.

The challenge of being a pastor's wife
    In my early years of being a mother, I realized I wanted to be a motivational speaker. I started doubting that I could be used to reach anyone, especially those who were broken. Why would I be so bold to put myself out there, only to be talked about and criticized? When I had freely taken abuse since childhood, dealt with depression, and now being a wife of a pastor, my self-esteem ultimately suffered even more.

ALL THE PREACHER'S WIVES
A Peek Behind The Curtain Of Being A Preacher's Wife

It was as if I was an abuse magnet and would never be able to reach others. I was too busy being broken in the church, knowing of God, but not knowing God.

Becoming fed up with feeling inadequate, I began reaching to God. The more I reached towards God, the more he was helping me to grow. I knew that my calling to be a motivational speaker was now turning into a desire to preach the gospel of Jesus Christ. Being told that if something happened to my pastor-husband, I would never become the pastor always rang in my head and pushed me to be a better me for the purpose of winning souls for the kingdom. I thrive on understanding that God has me here for a purpose.

Truth be told, being the wife of a preacher has not been all bad or all challenging. The greatest blessing that I received as a pastor's wife has been developing my personal growth in God through my relationship with Jesus Christ. For some reason, I spent the bulk of becoming a preacher's wife trying to understand where I fit in and wondered why I also felt challenged in a negative way with my husband-pastor and the congregation. I was constantly told that it was my responsibility to keep myself in a certain light. I had to look a particular way. I had to behave a certain way. I had not yet become a leader, and though I didn't have strong Biblical knowledge, I knew enough Christian songs to quote scripture like a scholar and I began studying the Word extensively.

Greatest Blessing as a Preacher's wife

Being a pastor's wife has been a door opener for me to walk into my destiny. I can speak to women about how God took me from a life of spiritual, mental, and physical abuse. God was preparing me for my calling in Him. I can speak to men from the standpoint of having a purpose and walking in with Godly boundaries, and most importantly, I can speak to children about not allowing the now to dictate the future. God has given me an open platform through ministry to win souls for His kingdom. God used my role as a pastor's wife to push me out in the forefront so that my insecurities won't hold me bound.

Final Words

To the pastors and their wives: **Marriage is your first ministry**. It is important to set boundaries. Not just for the sake of your marriage but for the sake of your sheep. When marriage is placed in the correct perspective, the little gap for the enemy to creep in is closed. I used to believe that a happy wife leads to a happy life. That couldn't be farther away from the truth. I now believe that a marriage, especially one in which the pastor and wife are in senior ministry, must be led by God and the Holy Spirit. My husband used to say, apart from God we have nothing, and we can do nothing. That saying is so true. It has only been through prayer and interceding that I can still say that I am a pastor's wife. What has kept me for over 14 years? It's knowing the word of God, and that the Bible has a defined order when it comes to marriage, that I choose to follow. God, your spouse, your children, and everything else.

Knowing that marriage is your first ministry outside of God, it is also as important to not only **know where your children fit in the equation**, but letting your children know as well. When children are placed in situations that they don't understand, we as parents cannot have the mentality that they are only children. The same way pastors and their wives experience a lot of church hurt; children experience it just as well. Children of pastors and their wives are just as vitally important to the church. They are required to dedicate time, effort, and energy, even in the early years, before they can make decisions for themselves. We must teach and be living examples to our children so that, as it is written, "even when he is old, he will not depart from it."

To the pastor's wives: For me, Sunday mornings could be very dreadful. Oftentimes, I didn't even want to get out of my bed to go to church and face the members of the congregation. I knew that if I didn't get up to go to church, I was setting a bad example for my girls. The truth of the matter is some days it may have been better for me to stay home because I was not only subjecting myself to the difficulties that I was facing, I was also not being a great support to my husband, and I was showing our children that it was OK to allow physical and mental situations to overshadow what God had been with my life. I was not a great example setter to my household family, nor was I being a great example setter to my church family. The term "first lady," in my view, means that you are not necessarily first to your spouse, but you are first to many women and children who should see you as a great leader.

It is inevitable that many days will be spent feeling lonely. Being lonely, however, is a part of ministry in which I believe God uses the pastor's wife as an intercessor for her pastor-husband. It is difficult to be a support to your husband when you are entangled in gossip and discourse in the church. It is also difficult to shepherd your sheep when they have an insight into the strength of how the food is being supplied to them. In layman's terms, that means it's difficult to pastor a flock when they have insight into your flaws and differences as the pastor's family. Not everyone can handle that their pastor is not perfect or that their pastor is just as human as he or she is.

You dress so tacky… Don't you care about how you look?... Pastor's wives are supposed to be dressed up and most of them wear hats. Where is your fancy hat? Getting all dressed up was one of the toughest tasks in ministry for me. Never was I a dressy/classy young lady, and I always desired to be that pastor's wife. At first, when I began feeling low and the real pain started hitting me, I started living in the mindset of "come as you are" and "they ought to be glad that I am here." It wasn't that I wanted to be defiant, I honestly didn't know how. I did not come from a privileged home, nor did I grow up desiring to be like the Jones. In my mind, once I changed who I had been all my life, it would change whom God designed me to be. I thought that because I was fearfully and wonderfully made, I needed to be alright with who and what I was. What I didn't take into consideration was that I wasn't only representing myself, I was a representation of God, my pastor-husband, and my children. It took me a long time to learn, but I learned that when I dressed as if I didn't care, I was not received in a way that others cared. It didn't take a rocket scientist or a lot of money for me to look nice. Not to mention, the nicer I looked, the better I felt. The better I felt, the more productive as a pastor's wife I became.

Preacher's wives, **you are a leader.** You don't have to be a world saver. When God called you to be a pastor's wife, He knew that you would lead by supporting your husband, as your husband would follow Him. There may be times in which you don't believe your husband is following Christ, this is when your prayers are most needed. You may not be a prayer warrior. You may not be a great singer, cook, or homemaker, but you are a leader in God's eyes. You have been called to cover your husband from and during tests and trials. When you hear the still voice letting you know God's desire for you as a pastor's wife, don't combat it. Pray to God, ask for direction, and remember that the people of the world are not your enemy.

ALL THE PREACHER'S WIVES
A Peek Behind The Curtain Of Being A Preacher's Wife

Pastor Patricia Jackson

"We would just like the negative perception of us to go away. Give us a chance. Be patient and give us the same grace and respect you want."

7
CAN YOU HANDLE MY TRUTH

This is who I am

To the readers of this chapter, I want you to know a little about me. I am a mother, grandmother, great-grandmother, Godmother, aunt, niece, and sister to many from another mother. I am a cousin, friend, entrepreneur, God's Messenger, Spiritual Mother, and a Pastor's wife. Yes, one might say I wear a lot of hats and I have to show up and function in all these positions on any given day. Philippians 4:13" gives me courage. "I can do all things through Christ that strengthens me".

What is this all about?

The trials of a pastor's wife are what this chapter is all about. Operating and functioning in the position of a pastor's wife can sometimes be one of the most challenging positions. How people introduce me or recognize me some days causes me to take a deep breath. Situations such as are you the Preacher's wife? Or hey, it's the wife of a Pastor. The whispers around corners *"that the Pastor's wife"* checking to see what you're buying in the grocery store while standing in the checkout lines. Most of the time our names are never mentioned. The position sometimes causes you to be nameless. We have a name.

ALL THE PREACHER'S WIVES
A Peek Behind The Curtain Of Being A Preacher's Wife

When you really give it some thought, no one woman wants to be introduced as that woman or she's so and so's wife. Think about it why do people address us as Pastor's wife? I would love for readers to know we are relevant, we show up every Sunday, and we are present. We would just like the negative perception of us to go away. Give us a chance. Be patient and give us the same grace and respect you want. The same forgiveness we give you, give it to us. We don't know everything. We are learning. Get to know us for yourself. Don't always believe everything you hear. I just believe if you would get to know us you would truly love us. If you prejudge us, you will never know the blessing we can be. Someone once told me to show up, shut up, and sit still with the 3 S's. If we are made to be silent you will never know us.

Let me be clear, I know everyone does not feel that way, but many do. I've seen other women join the church and are given all rights and benefits to choosing whatever position they want to serve in, in the church. They are welcomed by all. However, Pastor's wives are expected to sit and be silent. We don't get to tell or show who we are in the beginning, others describe who we are. Who we are, is told by others. *"A little leaven leaveneth the whole lump."* (Galatians 5:9) Our lives and the stories shared by others have made it so difficult for us. However, over time and prayer, we get to prove who we are. Thank God for Jesus.

Why I chose to be apart

When I was asked to share some of my journey as a preacher's wife, I said finally I get to tell the world who I am. I prayed to God for clarity. I then asked my husband for his permission and His prayers. I received clarity from God so then I asked myself, what parts of my life do I share? What can I share that will bless someone? What can I share that would not harm anyone? What not to share, because I would never want to hurt God's people or our Ministry. We live in a small town where everybody knows everybody, they know me, my husband, and our Ministry.

ALL THE PREACHER'S WIVES
A Peek Behind The Curtain Of Being A Preacher's Wife

How do I share my story and protect the guilty? We all know there are things that happen in our lives, and we can't share everything because we are all walking on different spiritual levels and some are not walking on any spiritual level. I would not want anyone to read anything into my truth that would bring harm and not help people to grow. Truth is some horrible things happened and it's not for all ears or eyes. I want you as a reader to realize we all make mistakes, but we take our mistakes and turn them into a blessing for all who will read this book. I believe that what the devil means for evil … Genesis 50:20. Some may have intended it to harm me, but God intended it for good to accomplish what is now be done, to the saving of many lives.

God chooses our Husband

God chooses the men of God. He anoints them and appoints them and presents them to the people as gifts. Jeremiah 3:15 says, *"Then will I give you shepherds after my own heart, who will lead you with knowledge and understanding."* He promises to give them knowledge and understanding and He watches over them. Sometimes the congregation forms an alliance against the wife. When the Man of God hears from God sometimes it is described that the wife makes the decision. I deem it an insult to God that someone will think that God will not honor his word and that the man who chose can't hear from Him and blame us for the correction, knowledge, and understanding given by God Himself. When our husbands make decisions, and you don't like them, take it up with God and pray. We don't deserve the backlash.

What I would like our Husband to know

We don't tell you everything, we just can't. There are things that happen that we must take to the Lord. We want you to be the best you can be for the Lord. You are the Good Shepherd and there are things that you don't need to know except God reveals them to you. We want you to be able to mount that pulpit every Sunday in the spirit and not in the flesh. We know how much you love us and yes you are our protector. We want you to preach from your heart and not look at

ALL THE PREACHER'S WIVES
A Peek Behind The Curtain Of Being A Preacher's Wife

Sis So or Brother so-and-so knowing they may have said something harmful to your wife or your children and yes you would be surprised how often that happens. Let me reassure you because it happens a lot in the Body of Christ.

When we do share, we want your heart to be open and situations to be addressed in the best interest of everyone, even if it means bringing correction and it's not received by the one receiving the correction, If correcting is necessary correct your wife in private and not from the pulpit or in the presence of others. We are willing to make the sacrifice. We are willing to support you on every hand and in every situation. We know you are sometimes stretched, and we will always be here for you. You are our Husband, and we're your help meets. We need you to hear our hearts. When you become overwhelmed with church matters, we still need you to hear us.

I pray for those who have yet to release their wives to do more; to extend them the freedom to be free and to release them to act through the influence of God and His will for the betterment of your family and the church despite what others think. Don't misunderstand what I'm writing. It's good over her, but it may not be good for some of my other sisters. Pastor hides most of their hurt but when you hurt and don't acknowledge it, we know, and we hurt with you. Remember, we were also chosen for this position. We are one. When you hurt, we hurt, so we know you know when we are hurting. Wives sometimes just need a simple "I don't know how to handle your pain so let's pray." I know the power of prayer will give strength to us and the ministry.

My prayer for the reader

I pray that those who read this book can see themselves as I see myself. I pray that people will have forgiveness for me as I have forgiven them. I pray my share will change someone's spiritual insight of what a Pastor's wife sometimes must endure on any given day of her life. I pray that people's negative opinions of others will be changed to positive ones, and if they see themselves in the book ask the father for forgiveness as I have. I pray that their personal feelings and thoughts going forth will be positive ones going forth. I stand on the word of God. Confess your faults one to another, and pray one for another, that ye may be healed; *"the effectual fervent prayer of the righteous availeth much."*

I was chosen for the position

As a Pastor's wife, I did not ask for this position. The thought never entered my mind. When I met my husband, I did not want to date him because he was an associate minister in his church. The same one he became a pastor in months later. I had seen so much bad treatment and heard so many horrible things spoken about other Pastors' wives, and I wanted no part of it. But God had other plans. Phone dates and in seven months I was his wife. Months later he became a Pastor. This let me know, we can say what we don't want or what we're not going to do, but we cannot abort the plan of God for our lives. From reading the word I do believe we were called from birth. I believe we are who we are before we enter our mother's womb based on the scripture in Jeremiah 1:5. The Lord said to Jeremiah, *"Before I shaped you in the womb, I knew all about you. Before you saw the light of day, I had holy plans for you; A prophet to the nations- that's what I had in mind for you."*

I was prepared for the Position

My siblings who are now all deceased often told my parents, I was their favorite and I always felt they were harder on me and had more restrictions on me. My siblings could do anything they wanted. I was always told you can't go. Mom would always say I need you to stay here with me. I was not allowed to go to any of the places they were allowed to go. I always had to go to church with my mom. One day my mom sat me down and said to me at the age of 13 and I quote she said they're not going to do all the things you're going to do. You're my miracle child. She said there will be places you will go that they are not going. She further shared with me that someone told her at birth that I was born with a veil over my face and that I was going to be used by God and she would have to always protect me. I was only 13 and that scared me. She said, *"Don't be afraid. God's hand will always be upon you and when you're afraid and don't know what to do, ask God to help you. I'll be here for you. I'm going to always watch over you."* In those days women were not free to exercise their gifts. My mom transitioned at the age of 52 and she had the gift of prophecy, I was young and did not know what it was. I did not understand her gift and didn't know what it was. I now know why so many people were drawn to her, all the phone calls and she was always talking and praying for them. My mom told me I was going to be able to see and do things that the other children would not be able to do. It was prepared for my journey to be used by God and step into the call of a Pastor's wife.

I chose to forget all the Preparation

I was with my mom all the time; I had seen so much during the years and gone through so much. I was ignorant of the gift and the journey that was ahead. When my mom transitioned, I chose to forget all the things my mom said to me because she was not here to share in my journey. I never stop serving God, but I did stray to try and forget the things I experienced with her. I had one of those you can run from the gift, but you can't hide. Eventually, I recognized you always end up starting from the place from which you stopped. I now know I was being prepared for this journey. I struggled in this role. There is no manual, role model, or mentor for such a position.

Best advice, if there is someone who desires to be a Preacher's wife make sure you're chosen, you have no idea the responsibility it holds. I pray that my share will bless you readers and it will give everyone a better understanding of the challenges we encounter while serving others and striving daily to please God.

It's an honor to serve God

It is an honor to serve but this position is not as glamorous as it may seem. As a Pastor's wife, I have had to face many trials, struggles, heartache, pain, and persecution. These 27 years have not always been easy as a matter of fact. On this journey, my road is just now becoming a little smoother; there are still those unexpected potholes. I still fall into a few from time to time.

In my earlier years as a Pastor's wife. it was much more challenging. My Sunday Mornings felt like Judgment Day. I do not consider myself a victim. I used my challenges, heartaches, tears, and pain to shape me into the Woman of God I am today. I came to the realization while praying one Sunday morning that there will always be opposition. Some people are settled in their ways and will not change their opinion of a preacher's wife.

I was a first-generation pastor's wife in a traditional church setting. I was a newlywed. I had no role model and no mentor. Prayer and trust in God were my teachers. I relied on the Holy Spirit for revealed knowledge. I was told to take advice from the seasoned women in the church. They could advise me; they knew the duties of a pastor's wife and what my position should entail.

My Truth! I did not receive any Godly advice. I was only instructed on how to dress, sit on the front row, smile, look cute, and just be quiet because that is what the pastor's wife does.

I am thinking in my mind that is going to be hard. I was so active in my previous church and did not know if I could adhere to that advice. Henceforth my Sunday morning became the most difficult day of the week for me because I wanted to participate.

My spirit man was so grieved. I did not just want to sit and do nothing. I am thinking Lord I am saved sanctified, filled with the spirit of God, and gifted with purpose, yet I'm not allowed to exercise my gift. How was this possible? I began taking baby steps, trying to be obedient to the order of the service. Think about it the enemy played his part if you know what I mean, constant taunting. I was trying not to let my feeling get the best of me. There were days when I felt like a specimen under a microscope. Maybe it was me in my feeling or maybe it was not me. It became so I just did not know how to please anyone. I isolated myself. I came in and went out quietly.

ALL THE PREACHER'S WIVES
A Peek Behind The Curtain Of Being A Preacher's Wife

Week after week all eyes positioned on me and what is she going to do today. When the battle became too much for me, I talked to my husband-pastor about some of the difficulties I was feeling. I thank God, he understood me and was compassionate toward my feelings. It was easy for him to understand me because there was a restriction placed on Him as well. He was not allowed to operate in the fullness of God. Some of the things God had called him to do were rejected. He was limited as well. We knew it was time to pray. The power of agreement we joined together in prayer. *"If two of you shall agree on earth touching anything that they shall ask, it shall be done for them of my father which is in heaven."* (Matthew 18:19).

The attacks on me were very personal and had nothing to do with the ministry most of the time. However, it did not take me long to realize that the things being done to me may have been personal, but I knew they were purposeful.

As a preacher's wife or a Christian at large, we must stay prayed up and understand *that "we know that all things work together for the good of those who love God, to those who are the called according to His purpose"* (Romans 8:28).

I stood on the word of God. *"No weapon formed against thee would be able to prosper and every tongue that rise against you in judgment thou shall condemn. This is the heritage of the servant of the Lord, and their righteousness is for me said the Lord."* (Isaiah 54:17)

I was pushed into the arms of the Lord. I prayed more than I had ever prayed. The more I prayed the stronger my relationship with Christ became. Pain and disappointment pushed me into purpose.

"Casting all our cares on Him for he cares for you is engraved in my heart" (1 Peter 5:7). I thank God for the persecution, the breaking, the crushing. The Oil will not come unless the olive is crushed. It provoked me into purpose.

Thank you, Jesus, I've learned how to *"Trust in the Lord with all my heart and lean not to my own understanding; In all thy ways acknowledge Him and He will direct my path"*. (Proverbs 3:5-6).

Every day is a lesson and so many things can and are happening you may not know what to do think or say. I don't believe people always know the impact of words, jester, or conversations with others can have such an impact on the mental and emotional being of others. I can say that because I know I've done it and have I asked for God's forgiveness, I will always have compassion for others,

There will always be adversity in the church, the whispering, the ugly looks, the unfair judgment, we just have to stay in a good relationship with God, walk in His will and in His ways and he will vindicate us. In every church, there are people from all walks of life and different levels of spiritual maturity, but at the end of the day I've learned I can't change people's reactions toward me, but I can and will be responsible for how I react to them.

ALL THE PREACHER'S WIVES
A Peek Behind The Curtain Of Being A Preacher's Wife

Coach Krystal Henry

"But one thing came clear quickly over my tenure as a leader: Your individual calling as a first lady will never fully mirror another First Lady."

ALL THE PREACHER'S WIVES
A Peek Behind The Curtain Of Being A Preacher's Wife

8
VIBRATIONS OF BROKEN SILENCE

"The pastor was preaching, and just as I was about to answer the call to discipleship to go to the front of the church, the pastor's wife called me over to her. She had an issue with my attire, she stated. Several other women joined her as she accused me of wanting the pastor and dressing provocatively to entice him. I was hurt, shocked, embarrassed, and angry. I was dressed in a suit that I wore to work all the time. I did not know there was anything wrong with my attire. They ambushed me out of nowhere! It was completely unexpected..."

The excerpt above is from my book, "Made To Lead Millions," Chapter 2, "Preparing to Lead." The first close encounter I had with a "First Lady" was when I was surrendering my life to the Lord. What is so interesting about this was that I grew up in a denomination that did not recognize the First Lady or have female ministers. So, this moment was really awkward for me and extremely unfamiliar. Yet, years later, I had no idea that God would call me to be a first lady. All my life, I had been leading; being involved in leadership (leading dance teams, cheerleading squads, and at work). So, I was very familiar with being a leader, however, being called to frontline leadership in ministry was never on my radar. In fact, being saved was not part of my plan either!

When I became a first lady, I had no idea fully what I would be encountering especially the different First Ladies I would be meeting and their unique mindsets. Some felt it was not their call, duty, or purpose to be a first lady, nonetheless, they found their passion in discipling and leading women, children, choirs, and full congregations into victory! But others chose not to be involved in the ministry at this level. There was a wide range of what leadership looked like as I looked to my fellow contemporaries for direction, understanding, and guidance. But one thing came clear quickly over my tenure as a leader: Your individual calling as a first lady will never fully mirror another First Lady.

The definition of a leader is one who influences, empowers, builds, trains, and establishes others to succeed! Proverbs 14:1, states, *"A wise woman builds her house, but the foolish pulls it down with her hands."* Behind and beside successful pastors are First Ladies that build their homes, families, and ministries. If you know your husband is your soulmate and you are his rib, then God has chosen you to be a leader of leaders! No matter what your title is, you are the head of the church, therefore, wisdom, character, commitment, and responsibility are crucial.

When God gave us "Power of the Gospel Ministries," we were called to do everything! My husband and I have been married for 26 years. And after four years of marriage, God called my husband to be a pastor. With this calling, I became a first lady.

God moved quickly in our ministry. We were first-generation pastors and first lady and have been serving the Lord for over 22 years. When I prophesied to my husband that he was going to be a pastor, he struggled with the idea. Now, when God told me this, it never dawned on me that I would be a first lady! Nor did it cross my mind the extent that we would yield ourselves to the body of Christ. It did not matter if we were perfect or not, God called us. Perfection is not what God called us to, but obedience. When I looked at the Bible and realized that no one was perfect except, The Father, the Son, and the Holy Ghost, then I resolved, I can be used by God.

The closer we got to the LORD; the more God revealed to us that He was calling us to pastor. And according to II Peter 1:10, we found out also that our call and election must be made sure. It was a non-negotiable election! The definition of election in this verse means that God has chosen you, and He has the first, last, and final vote. Non-negotiable is your calling also! When God calls you into service it is like when He changed Abram's name to Abraham. Abram went from a father of none to a father of many nations. The God-given name change came with new responsibilities, purpose, and the promise of a secured destiny.

Diligence increases the more you come into the knowledge and understanding of your call and election! Diligence is not just what you do, or how many times you do it, but it is your continued persistence. Diligently seeking HIM happens through tests, good days, victories, whispers, miracles, and rejections. As well, becoming a woman that diligently seeks HIM, becomes a part of who you are. A woman who faithfully trusts in the LORD will also be that first lady whose husband's heart will safely trust in her. With these qualities, the pastor will be able to entrust his first lady with their marriage, family, and ministry!

The "First Lady" title is not biblical. Many people argue that a First Lady is only married to the Pastor, therefore, she does not deserve power or honor. In addition, we use titles such as Pope, Archbishop, Cardinal, Chief-Apostle, and Usher, which are titles that are not biblically based either, yet these positions are part of the 21st-Century church. I believe no matter what the title is, God has anointed us on purpose. I posed the question, years ago, why do we ordain, apostles, pastors, evangelists, prophets, and not teachers? Ephesians 4:11 names all these specific biblically based titles yet, man traditionally chose to ordain four.

ALL THE PREACHER'S WIVES
A Peek Behind The Curtain Of Being A Preacher's Wife

As a first lady, you have been enlisted in "The Secret Service of Silence. Although the title is not described in the Bible, it does you well to learn how to operate in Self-Control, Love, Prayer, Intercession, Peacemaking Skills, and warring in the spirit. Fortunately, this is not "Mission Impossible" like in the movies, but this assignment is very possible, and you can do it!

When I began operating as a first lady, God took me to the following scripture: Ephesians 6:12 *"For we do not wrestle against flesh and blood, but against principalities, against powers, against the rulers of darkness of this age, against spiritual hosts of wickedness in the heavenly places."* I felt a weight on the need to study this scripture. In 2009, it became apparent why God wanted me to study this scripture.

One day I was out shopping looking for a dress for our Marriage Retreat, which was held on Valentine's Day Eve, February 13, 2009. At this point, we had been conducting the retreats for years. So, as I was showering and preparing to adorn myself with a beautiful red dress, I found a lump near my collarbone. Immediately, I asked my husband if he felt and saw what I saw, and he did!

My last mammogram was in December just a few months before and everything was fine. Therefore, I pushed my fear down and out of my mind so that we could have an amazing weekend. Regardless, I knew I needed to go to my doctor.

It took me weeks to get an appointment. When I went back to my doctor, she saw and felt the same thing. She sent me to have another mammogram. I did, and the lump was getting bigger day by day.

The doctor that read my mammogram came in personally to speak to me. He apologized and assured me that there was nothing there in December. At this point, I could see the lump protruding under my skin. So next, a lumpectomy was scheduled. It took six weeks to be seen. By this time, the lump had grown at a rate of 83%. After my appointment, my breast surgeon came into the recovery room and explained that she knew she got the whole tumor and removed some lymph nodes for testing. She said that my tumor was shaped in a perfect circle and was not cancerous because of its shape. Then, she scheduled a follow-up visit to go over the lab results.

My husband accompanied me to the visit with my breast surgeon. I sat there in silence as I heard the word, "CANCER!" She began to cry and stated that she had almost thrown away my tumor because they are taught most cancerous tumors usually have tenacles or spread out awkwardly. My tumor was perfectly round like a large marble or gumball. It had quickly progressed from stage II to III by April. My situation was so unique that I was even used as a case study because of the unusually aggressive nature of my triple-negative breast cancer.

After hearing this, thoughts of my grandmother dying of Cancer seeped into my mind! My husband grabbed my hand as we listened to the doctor. And with all the strength and faith within me, I told my doctor that I was going to be fine. She explained the rounds of chemotherapy, and radiation therapy, and scheduled the oncologist I would see in a few weeks. Not one tear dropped. Yes, The War was on! We were thirteen years into our marriage at this point and we were facing death head-on!

My family had different responses to the diagnosis of cancer. I phoned my mom and she said she sat in a corner the entire day crying. I did not tell my son anything until my fifth day after chemotherapy. You see, you will lose your hair around the seventeenth to the twentieth day after your first round of chemo. But I knew I would have to tell him, so he would not be shocked. Our 6-year-old son told me he was going to pray to God, and I would be healed. My husband went upstairs and played his video game. This was his therapy of silence. So, I fought physically with medicine and my family's support.

ALL THE PREACHER'S WIVES
A Peek Behind The Curtain Of Being A Preacher's Wife

The effects of the chemotherapy were like wrestling with my flesh, blood, people, principalities, powers, darkness, and death. God assured me with the following statement, although "breast cancer is a silent killer, I would not be a silent survivor!" It was at that moment that I knew that I was going to live! I was being made a warrior for God's glory. My combat as a First Lady was against the enemy of fear, doubt, and death.

I declared everywhere I went, that I would not be a "silent survivor!" My God-therapy began with posted notes everywhere! I decreed I will live and not die! I had the work of the Lord to do. All things were going to work together for my good because I love the Lord and am called according to His purpose.

These declarations and the decrees were in my car, at my desk at work, in my bathroom on the mirrors, in my closet, and at church in the pastor's office. I listened to worship music, chapters of the Bible, prayers on YouTube, and studied scriptures on healing. I prayed God's Word back to HIM and believed I would live. My focus was LIFE! This was my God-therapy that I needed to recover.

It was like I could hear the worst-case scenarios running through everyone's minds, even our church members. Repeatedly, these sad faces came up to me, rubbed my arm, and said, "I am praying for you." Finally, I had to tell the congregation, coworkers, family, and friends, "If you cannot be positive, speak life, and share laughter and love, then please stay away. If you cannot believe with me, do not come to me crying about my tribulation. If I am not crying, you cannot cry either. Do not bring the spirit of death to me! I rebuked death in Jesus' Name."

Also, I knew silently my husband was afraid of death. He had only been in the hospital once in his lifetime. The family and friends he knew were all alive. Death was not something he was accustomed to dealing with. In fact, I felt the spirit of death lurking in the shadows. I could especially feel death around those who were waiting for me to die.

I began receiving invitations to different events speaking out against death, dread, and cancer -- speaking life and praying for others to LIVE and not DIE! Then a young lady who encouraged me through my chemotherapy process died. In fact, she lost her battle with cancer. She left behind three children under ten and a husband. It was her second battle in less than five years. That shook me. Death came even closer that day as tears began to fall.

Being a first lady and doing any other acts or activities associated with a "First Lady" was the last thing on my mind during this time in my life. However, no matter what challenges you might be going through as a first lady in a church, there is always an undercurrent of expectations that members still desire from you. Perhaps, this is one of the areas that leadership often overlooks when stepping into a position as pastor of a church. If there is a male counterpart called to pastor a church, you better believe that the wife is called also. And when the wife does not do all that is expected of her, there will be gossip and backlash whether it is overt or insidious. Now, of course, this is not everyone, but this is a part of the equation.

One day, the thought of life not standing still had my focus, when I heard my son exclaim from the back seat, "I want to take Communion!" His dad refused. You see, we prefer that disciples understand why they receive Communion. Our son asked again why he could not receive communion. As a preacher's kid you do not realize that they are really hearing what you are teaching, preaching, and living. My son debated his father well and won. We set up classes for him and a few others to prepare for communion and baptism training.

At this point in my life, I felt like the enemy delayed and detoured powerful monumental moments from me, because of my bout with

ALL THE PREACHER'S WIVES
A Peek Behind The Curtain Of Being A Preacher's Wife

Cancer. The baptism of our son and my ordination were postponed. Although I remained silent, disappointment tried to creep in and steal my joy.

I learned that I could no longer look into the faces of the people around me. I understood, it was not them, but the spirit operating in them. My boss, my coworkers, family, church members, and random people would frustrate me. People would say, "If I were you, I would have done such and such or I would not take that!" My frustrations grew to the point that I felt I needed deliverance.

Our ninth church anniversary was approaching. The congregation prepared for the celebration. This was the first year we were not involved in the planning. The congregation wanted to surprise us and give us a break. We were excited to see what they were going to do.

We celebrated our wedding anniversary on August 31st, our salvation anniversary on September 1st, and the church anniversary on September 10th. Our family would also take a weeklong vacation around this time before our son's school year started. This was a point in time when I really needed a break!

Our congregation told us to not buy anything for our celebration service, to not even come up to help with decorations. So, we relaxed and let them do their thing! We arrived at church with excitement, and they ushered us to the Pastor's Office where we were to dress and wait for the service to begin. My husband was given a navy and light blue striped suit, shoes, accessories, and cologne. His cuff links were exceptional. I was like --wow, love, you look great! He strutted around the office like he was Mr. It! We just laughed. I had not realized I had not laughed in a while.

Then my attire arrived. I could not believe it! Needless to say, I was extremely disheartened. I was 42 and looked younger than my age. The dress they brought me was for a much more mature first lady as well as the two-inch-low heels were too big and atrocious. They provided no accessories or perfume. While I was extremely disappointed, I remained silent and just smiled.

Once we were separately escorted into the sanctuary, I was shocked and bewildered by their color choices which clashed on every level. Our church colors are purple, black, gray, and silver. The attire they selected for us was blue and white. The decorations were orange, hot pink, and lime green. The theme was the fruit of the spirit. They gave us a basket of nine pieces of fruit and a grand presentation on what each fruit represented. The scripture reference was from Galatians 5:22-23 which states, *"But the fruit of the Spirit is love, joy, peace, forbearance, kindness, goodness, faithfulness, gentleness, and self-control. Against such things, there is no law."*

They invited other congregations to join in on the celebration. We were served dinner and cake. My husband thought they were going to follow up with some type of love offering based on nine years of service and the fact we have never received a salary.

By the end of the night, I was angry. Again, I found myself wrestling against flesh and blood. God was not only testing my body and mind but my attitude as well. When I look back on this situation now, truly, He was preparing me for more! My calling as a first lady was bigger than me and this position.

My husband used to laugh at me when I would say you made me mad. "Oh, you are giving me that much power to make you mad." It takes self-control to not react or act out the way your flesh wants to at times. We are responsible for how we act, our character, what we say, how we conduct the work of the ministry, and labor of love for the Kingdom of God or lack thereof. I needed the fruit of the spirit in this ninth year!

ALL THE PREACHER'S WIVES
A Peek Behind The Curtain Of Being A Preacher's Wife

My beauty was fleeting. Chemotherapy caused black spots to show up on the palms of my hands and the soles of my feet. My skin was burned by radiation. I lost all my hair everywhere. I gained weight and was weak. It was time for me to discover what God wanted me to learn. Then, He led me to the word "meekness."

Meekness is self-control, strength in my weakness, quietness, and humbleness in dominion. In Hebrew, the word is anvah which means not easily provoked. It is our responsibility to operate by the Holy Spirit and not according to the flesh. Jesus was meek not weak because He had all power to destroy everything, yet He had mercy on us.

Here are two more scriptures that helped me get an understanding of this when I was processing everything that was going on in my life during this time. *"I will leave in your midst A meek and humble people, and they shall trust in the name of the LORD"* (Zephaniah 3:12). And *"But the meek shall inherit the earth and shall delight themselves in the abundance of peace"* (Psalms 37:11). The meekness of God became implanted in me; therefore, I allowed the Holy Spirit to temper me instead of allowing my flesh to rise in anger; fighting or fussing.

My attack was coming from every side like in a dream I had of the wolves in sheep's clothing. I was standing in a very green meadow with beautiful white sheep all around me. As they came nearer and nearer, I recognized long fluffy tails coming from underneath the white wool. Sharp teeth came into focus as they lunged and began to bite, nip, and attack me! That meant those that were supposed to be meek, and caring were going to be biting and causing me to bleed. Predators attack the weaker animals. The ones that are sick, young, old, or alone. My God-therapy comforted me during my weak periods as the wolves in sheep's clothing attacked me. Although nothing prepared me for what I encountered one Bible Study.

I made it to Bible study one night after a long ride through traffic. I had no idea what topic they would be discussing, but boy was I shocked! They were discussing, "who would replace the First Lady after she was gone." I can't tell you the pain and anguish I felt sitting there as they discussed my pending demise.

They addressed whether should it be a woman from inside or outside the church. Examples from their past experiences, other churches, and references from my current battle with cancer were discussed. Our Bible studies usually dealt with current headline issues or topics that someone may be struggling with in the church, but certainly nothing like this. I sat on the back row listening to the different variations of my replacement. And just so you know, all the leaders were present and participating.

Anger rose inside of me as I listened to this rhetoric. How could they feel comfortable enough to have this discussion? I am here and alive! Then I heard, "Let the peace that passes all understanding guard your heart and mind in Christ Jesus according to Philippians 4:7." So, I remained SILENT. Meekness replaced my anger with SILENCE. After Bible study, I went home and continued this SILENCE for years.

When I was first diagnosed with breast cancer, God said, "Breast cancer is a Silent Killer, but you will not be a SILENT SURVIVOR!" I survived much trepidation during this testing period of my battle with the spirit of cancer, death, fear, anger, doubt, and tribulations. I surfaced like the eagle described in Isaiah 40:31, which states,

> *"But those who wait on the LORD*
> *Shall renew their strength;*
> *They shall mount up with wings like eagles,*
> *They shall run and not be weary,*
> *They shall walk and not faint."*

My journey during this period, as a First Lady, in the natural, was truly a tumultuous season for me, but in the spirit, God made me

ALL THE PREACHER'S WIVES
A Peek Behind The Curtain Of Being A Preacher's Wife

resilient. I held onto this scripture, and it became a reality for me, especially when I heard the story of the eagles' mid-life crisis. Some say it does not happen; others say it does. The story depicts the fortieth year of the eagle. His beak gets too heavy, and their claws become too long. They must beat their beak off and pull their talons out. Afterward, their talons and beak would grow back better. Healthy eagles were known to drop food down to the grounded ones for their survival. This painful process was an obstacle that must be overcome for the eagle to potentially live another 30 years.

My cancer crisis was like the eagle crisis. I was in my forties. I lost my hair; my skin was damaged by radiation, my body fought against chemotherapy, and my mind battled offenses from the enemy through people. Through it all, God's will prevailed.

So now, I am not a Silent Survivor. The vibration of my voice broke my silence so that the words of my testimony will bring you to a risen position. My prayer is that we will rise and break the silence together, walk in the power of meekness, deliver new measures of faith, accept the purposeful lessons, and render mercy to those who need it, in Jesus' name. AMEN!

First Ladies, let the vibrations of our voices rise together!!!

Tenelle Torrence

"You don't have to tell them any and every detail for them to pray for you. You just have to tell them you want them to pray for you and your marriage."

9
UNDERSTANDING THE MARRIAGE ASSIGNMENT

As I place my heart in the position to write these words, all I am encapsulating is healing for the hearts. The ministry of healing is simultaneous and synonymous with the ministry of marriage. My journey and intersection in this grace, space, and time has seen me being married to a pastor for 19 years, divorced, and now remarried to a man and minister of God for almost 3 years while I have the privilege to serve others as a pastor. This life has been full of healing moments. So, for me, I see marriage as a healing assignment. It has allowed the Lord to show me how much he has loved me, how much he has forgiven me, and how much he has given me.

Healing is the Marriage Assignment!

When you are able to minister to each other in the spotlight of others, this is the essence and actionable work of healing as you magnify the will of God in your lives. In the Hebrew context, the word for healing is marpe (mar-pay). It means healing, cure, and health. Healing with the intent of absolute remedy. Marriage is an absolute remedy for the heart of mankind. It is this mystery of how two can become one. Marriage within the placeholder of ministry leaders must be one AND at the same exemplify oneness in your atmosphere of influence. This restoration carries the weight of national affliction in its assignment. The marriage assignment is the foundation of your hearts, your homes, your states, and your nations. What entity shows children how to treat each other? What union has been challenged by altered laws? What peace treaty shows the love of God for us in a human way? Marriage. Our marriages must live in a state of healing to be impactful in the kingdom of God.

Malachi 4:2 says, "But unto you that fear my name shall the Sun of righteousness arises with **healing** in his wings, and ye shall go forth and grow up as calves of the stall." This is the healing and restoration that grows and multiplies the love of God in our surroundings. This love shoulders one understanding that God's name is represented in even the name you share in your marriage. You know that when we get married, we share a last name; however, when we unify in marriage, we share the name of our spouse and the name of the Lord! For the fear and reverence of our Lord Jesus Christ is in our name. That became a golden nugget for me.

Mind the Business of Your Name!

In ministry, I had to mind the business of our name in the kingdom of God. Our name represents our destiny and kingdom assignment. And in "mind", I had to intentionally lift up our shared name in God's affirmations, in God's word, and in my prayers with God. This ushers oneness to esteem us as one purpose, one mind, one heart, one hand, one foot, and one tongue to proclaim the word of God. In unity there is healing and a state of healed. This is the vulnerability of marriage in ministry. Marriage reveals individual hearts, agendas, plans, shortcomings, successes, and thoughts. To be in a lifestyle of healed renders you to be on a continuous assignment of being ONE.

Your Words For Your Marriage are an OR (Operating Room) Moment!

Healing in the Hebrew also *signifies* healing of the tongue and profit. Proverbs 18:21 (KJV) speaks that "death and life are in the power of the tongue, and they that love it shall eat the fruit thereof." When we speak about our marriage and our spouses, we are either speaking about life or death. There is nothing in between that we can speak. It is death or life we speak and nothing else. There is no gray area, but every word that is spoken gives life or death and not one thing else. Think about life OR death. Now picture having this life-saving power in an operating room. Every time you say a word, you are sending it out to be an instrument in this operating room. It will administer prosperity or harm. Your words and actions must only support life-giving words to ourselves, our spouses, and our marriages. Life words come from a heart that beats forgiveness.

As long as we live, we will be human beings striving for perfection and maturity. In the strive, there are times in life when there are missed moments, missed important events, missed emotions, missed words, and missed actions that could lead to miscommunication within a marriage. As the missing pieces try to cause aggravation, we must forgive ourselves and each other. When you let forgiveness flow from your heart you release the pain of suffering from yourself and from others.

This is the mystery of marriage. The power of marriage allows forgiveness to heal your heart and to proclaim God's word. As you walk as one, practice forgiveness so that you may be able to release hurt and misunderstandings and allow love to grow and not die. So many times, I've heard people say you are my ride or die. In this, I declare that your spouse is your ride and life partner.

Yield not Willed!

Another Hebrew meaning for healing is yielding, wholesome, and tangible deliverance. The fullness of marriage brings about submission. When you submit, you submit to the will and purpose of God for your marriage. You find yourself in the strength of willfully joining in the plan of God. Someone once told me that it takes a strong person to submit by choice. Submission carries no manipulation or control.

Submission can't be willed on someone else. Each person must decide to submit, and agree, without ultimatums, threats, or fear of retaliation. When I realized that submission was to God and showed the character of grace, I thrived in this area. Also, I noticed in Ephesians 5 that each person should submit themselves to each as unto the Lord, and then Paul says, look wives yield to your own husband. Pay special attention to the order of your marriage and surrender attention, time, and effort to the land that the Lord has given you.

Yielding to the care and maintenance of your land mandates that we tend our land with prayers. We must uproot any negative words or festering feelings by first praying for ourselves. When we pray for ourselves first, we are telling God that we know that in every situation, the only truly righteous one is Him. We set aside prejudices, prepositioned attitudes, and misplaced priorities. We admit that we can only yield to the presence of the Lord.

Pray For Yourself as You Pray for Your Spouse!

We can then pray for God to remove any tares that may have been planted in our hearts. We can pray for the perfect will of God as we allow Him to minister to His ministry in us. Sometimes in prayer, you may have been guilty of thinking that your prayer would just slay all the things you had deemed as wrong thinking, toxic acting, or demonic activity out of your mate's life and of your marriage. But when you go to God in prayer for who He is in YOU, you have declared that you will face your own demons, chaotic ideas, or generational motives above all else. Our whole experience must be released in prayer so that we may have a complete life with our spouse.

I remember one of those prayer days. I was frustrated by a situation that arose between me and my spouse. I went to God with some of those words you should not use or ingrain in your mind. I was saying, "He never does what he says. He always does what he wants without considering the cost. He does not love me." I heard a small, still, sovereign voice says, "Do you love him?" I was appalled by that question but yet knew that this had to be my God speaking to me. So, I started asking God to heal my heart, help me be humble to him, and then I could be humble to my spouse. God brought attention to my heart in the situation first. He will do this every time you open yourself up for complete forgiveness, reconciliation, and ultimately love. Whose love am I referring to? I am speaking of God's love, God's forgiveness, and God's reconciliation. This also keeps you from having a victim mentality in prayer. How about an inner vow that is fruitful? Tell yourself, I will always pray for myself and my spouse!

Be Accountable for the Love of God in Your Marriage!

You must also request to pray with your spouse if that is not currently taking place. The Bible says that one can chase 1000 and two can chase 10,000. Agree on a designated time and location to pray.

Make sure it is the most convenient and natural time to pray. When you wake up or when you go to bed is a great time to pray. Pray prayers of love and unity. You know what I mean. If your in-law is saying negative things to you, then you could pray for your hearts to be softened, for forgiveness, for all things to work together for your good, or for the enemy's strategies to be identified and stopped by the blood of Jesus. You don't have to pray that your in-law "enemy" will die if they continue to speak negative words. This is not a prayer, because it is not seasoned with the love of Christ. This will surely cause further disruption and make your spouse stop praying with you.

Now, these prayer strategies are necessary for every couple. As a matter of fact, all of these words I am sharing from my heart can benefit any marriage. This is a strategy that spouses of people in ministry must master. For the prayers allow peace to remain, it open doors of communication, and it fortifies your mind from the bombardment of sickly thoughts. But what sets this apart is the idea that you should have a praying community. This is the moment thoughts that can make your marriage malnutritioned and lacking can appear.

These thoughts can take over and tell you that there is NO ONE who could or would support you in prayer or counsel with your marriage. Your husband is too well-known. Your issue is different. Your situation is too embarrassing and you just can't be looked at this way.. You can't see how this would help you to overcome your marriage. Remember you don't have to tell anyone the situation or detail.

Revelations 12:11 states that you overcome in your lives by the blood of the Lamb, and by the word of your testimony and that you don't love your life unto death. Does this mean I can overcome my testimony in marriage as well? Is there any way you can guard your marriage and not expose your marriage to the devil? I know it is!

When considering a praying community to surround you, it might be another trusted couple, spiritual guidance, or trained and spiritual marriage counseling. The people must be Holy Spirit filled with intentions of restoration for both people. Wise counsel is in the bible and could be found in some bible-based books. I compel you to seek out wise counsel in the bible, biblical resources, and godly human counsel to be accountable to the love of God in your marriage.

Options to be accountable to strengthen your marriage could be prayer warriors, counselors, marriage groups, and Bible-based marriage book studies. All of these options look very different, offer varied settings, and carry a wealth of tools and strategies for your marriage. But all of them require the guidance, leading, and inspiration of the Holy Spirit and agreement within your marriage. Some couples have individual prayer partners whom they agreed to pray for what they are willing to share. You don't have to tell them every detail or any detail for them to pray for you. You just have to tell them you want them to pray for you and your marriage. I suggest praying with other married individuals. You do have some seasoned women who may be widowed that could be your fit for a prayer partner.

Let The Holy Spirit Instruct You!

The Holy Spirit will guide you to your perfect, God-purposed person who will pray and/or counsel with the honor and integrity of Jesus' blood-bought covenant agreement for you and your marriage. Some things I experienced that were helpful were praying together, a couple being our prayer partners, marriage peer book group discussions, independent marriage book study with my spouse, and a weekend marriage retreat to renew commitment. The Lord actually blessed us in that the retreat had a special session with pastors and wives in ministry to have a separate session. This was unique in that it allowed for a safe space to share experiences and gather biblical tools to fortify the marriage. To find these options, pray for Holy Spirit to guide you to the best healing and empowering way for you and your spouse.

No Blame Game or Shame Game!

I love to study the events surrounding our first pastor and wife. You know them to be Adam and Eve. Adam and Eve only had one commandment to follow to don't eat of the tree of the knowledge of good and evil. I looked up the number of different fruit-bearing trees there are currently and google said it was 27 different fruit trees in the world. Let's just say there were 28 fruit-bearing trees and Eve had to eat the fruit off of the one tree God said to not eat. I have heard so many Bible interpretations of why Eve ate the fruit such as she was tricked by the snake, she was weak, and she was seeking Adam's attention. I have also heard reasons presented of why Adam ate the fruit as he wanted to cover Eve, he didn't want Eve to be separated from him, or Adam was just weak too. Sometimes when we try to find a reason for why we sinned, we decide to assign blame to ourselves or to someone else. Blame is not necessary, but accountability is. When you blame it is always a reason and it renders someone helpless and someone as the guilty party. Remember, you are not a victim! What God is seeking is accountability to say, Lord, I sinned, and I ask for your forgiveness. When you stop blaming you are in a position to be forgiven for the disobedience and to be restored.

Blame also brings shame to ourselves or our spouses and shame tends to bring more blame. It is a violent tornado that will destroy anything in its pathway. Shame will even make you hide, blame some more, and cover-up.

Genesis 3:7-13 (KJV)

"And the eyes of them both were opened, and they knew that they were naked, and they sewed fig leaves together and made themselves aprons. And they heard the voice of the Lord God walking in the garden in the cool of the day: and Adam and his wife hid from the presence of the Lord God amongst the trees of the garden. And the Lord God called unto Adam, and said unto him, Where art thou? And he said, I heard thy voice in the garden, and I was afraid because I was naked; and I hid. And he said, who told thee that thou wast naked? Hast thou eaten of the tree, whereof I commanded thee that thou shouldest not eat? And the man said, The woman whom thou gavest to be with me, she gave me of the tree, and I did eat. And the Lord God said unto the woman, what is this that thou hast done? And the woman said, the serpent beguiled me, and I did eat."

For this is what Adam and Eve did. They were ashamed of eating the forbidden fruit. They hid from their God. They hid from their love, and they covered up. Adam blamed Eve. Eve blamed the snake. And they were ashamed and separated from God. However, accountability assigns the sin as unacceptable. This allows you to run to God for cover. This takes away your failed attempt to run away from God. For whom can truly run from God? So, Run to God! Go to your opportunity to be cleansed from all unrighteousness, unhealthy thinking, and ungodly actions. Then God's forgiveness helps us to decide to go out and sin no more.

So in marriage when situations happen, when decisions are made, when disappointments or missed appointments occur, don't look for whom to blame. Seek accountability and righteous standing with God. If you didn't make the decision that was not best, but your spouse, this mindset will release you to pray with love and clarity. For God is the only righteous one who knows all and is perfect in all His ways. This gives us an abundance of grace for one another.

Above All Else Agree!

Don't just seek agreement but agree! Amos 3:3 says, "Can two walk together, except they are agreed?" Just imagine that you two are one and you are in one physical body. You both have one leg to operate. If you move one leg, but the other leg is still, the entire body will not move far or move quickly. If one leg is moving forward and the other is moving backward, the body will split. This depicts clearly how you must communicate and have an agreement for both people or legs to move forward in their goals and lives.

So, what should two people in a marriage agree on? You want agreement on faith, finances, and family needs and assignments to identify just a few areas of agreement. Agreement happens when you decide to agree with God, agree with God in yourself, and agree with God in you and your spouse. If you are already married, it is never too late to agree. If you are thinking about marrying someone with the calling of a shepherd or pastor, you want to clearly communicate your intentions and yourself before saying, I do. I saw in Genesis 24 and verses 55-59 where Rebekkah was asked if she wanted to go with Abraham's servant to be joined to Isaac. Rebekkah's mother and brother asked her if she wanted to go to Isaac and his family and his God. She answered yes. Always remember before saying yes, you have a responsibility to yourself to ask yourself, is this my husband that I can submit to in the name of God and honor him and only him all the days of my life? I pray that you have a discerning heart to see what is truly in your heart and in his heart. So when God answers you, you are willing and prepared to be his wife. Rebekkah did not hesitate or stall. I believe she had to agree with God's will for your life before this question was even presented to her. When you know who God has made you then you can agree to God's will for your life joined with another. Agreement with God solves issues within your marriage so that you won't go to sleep angry with your spouse. Agree to agree with God's sovereignty and perfect will above anything else in your life.

Heart Thoughts for Your Heart Actions!

One last nugget is Proverbs 23:7 that says that so as a man thinketh in his heart, so is he. I had an open vision where I was laying down and I could see my heart responding to every thought in me. As my heart reacted, I could see sound waves going out from my heart to every nerve in my body. The waves were colorful and they lit up my body as the word waves made it to every area of my body.

As the waves went out, I could hear the words of love, hope, and faith. God's word is true. Whatever we think and meditate on, we become. So, for your marriage, make your heart think of words that will illuminate you and your spouse. Some thoughts to think and act on are:

ALL THE PREACHER'S WIVES
A Peek Behind The Curtain Of Being A Preacher's Wife

Heart Thoughts	Heart Actions
Don't go to sleep angry	Pray for you to accept God' will, pray to be a vessel for God, and communicate in God's timing with your spouse. If you are likely to pull away from your spouse during hard times, make a list of how you pull away and commit to not doing some of those items. Then mature to not doing any of those responses. If you are talkative, make a list of what you could do instead of overtalking an issue. Bring up the subject after praying and asking God what to say and when to say it.
Agree quickly	Pray for God to give you any righteous area to agree on in the matter. Ex. You want to invest, and your spouse wants to have an emergency fund. Look at it as a blessing! You both want to prosper, and you pray for God to speak to you both on how to prosper.
Avoid negative words or inner vows about your spouse	Don't use words like you "never" or you "always". Ex. You never listen. You always forget about what I think.
Be Accountable to love	Find accountability measures that fit your marriage style. Ex. prayer partners, prayer couples, group book discussions on marriage.
Commit to enjoying the journey of life with your spouse (Ride and Live and stop thinking in terms of ride and dying in your relationship.	Go on dates, spend time alone and don't talk about any responsibilities, especially church.

So, agree to have a prosperous and healed marriage. Agree with God that you shall live and not die and therefore your marriage shall live and not die to declare the works of The Lord! For your healing, your marriage, your assignment in heaven depends on you loving your spouse. Let the Holy Spirit comfort you. Yes, some days, you will need comforting, and your spouse will too. Let the Holy Spirit give you the words to guard your heart and make you accountable to fighting in the spirit with faith for your marriage. It's your will to submit. It's your marriage to maintain and to thrive. It's your love to grow!

ALL THE PREACHER'S WIVES
A Peek Behind The Curtain Of Being A Preacher's Wife

TreSonya Madison Durden

"According to my husband, he knew instantly that I would be his wife. But I "friend-zoned" him, and we remained friends for over six years."

ALL THE PREACHER'S WIVES
A Peek Behind The Curtain Of Being A Preacher's Wife

10
ONE PLUS ONE EQUALS ONE

The Bible teaches, *"Two are better than one, because they have a good return for their labor."* In the beginning, God created Adam and Eve. He gave a direct order to them to fill the earth and master it. Specifically, God has ordained the human race to fulfill His plan to replenish the earth. *"And God blessed them, and God said unto them, Be fruitful, and multiply, and replenish the earth, and subdue it: and have dominion over the fish of the sea, and over the fowl of the air, and over every living thing that moveth upon the earth."* We all know the story.

As with many young little girls, I could not wait to get older to have a family. I remember thinking, "I'm going to be the best person, wife, and mother ever." When you look back over your life, I am sure you thought of ways you wanted to be a better person as well. As women, it is in our nature to want what is best. We are like that by Divine design. There are times, though, because of life's up and down experiences, that we wonder if God truly wants the best for us. However, once we sincerely open up, allow God in our hearts, and put all our trust in Him without doubting, we are able to see a little clearer His desire for us to become better individuals through whom His light will shine to draw others to Him.

Ultimately, the decision was mine. It was I and I alone who said those three little letters that would change my life forever. "Y-E-

ALL THE PREACHER'S WIVES
A Peek Behind The Curtain Of Being A Preacher's Wife

S!" I could not even imagine what impact those three small letters would eventually have on my life. I had no idea of the developmental journey ahead for me in the request of getting married and my longing for the person God ordained specifically for my life. There were not only certain areas for improvements with my husband, but the shocking and surprising reality was the recognition and acknowledgement about myself as well. However, it is a normal desire for women to want to get married. It is God's original plan for man and woman to come together as one — *"and the two shall become one flesh."*

In the Beginning…

"A preacher's wife?" This is the question I asked God once I realized that life as I knew it was about to change right before my eyes. Even though I grew up in a small town, I really did not have a true, personal relationship with the pastor's wife, the "First Lady" of my childhood church. Once I became an adult and joined a church in another city, there again, I did not have a relationship with the First Lady of the church. There were so many people always crowded around her, and since I was a person that did not really like a lot of people around me, I basically chose not to get close to the First Lady. So, all of my life, I had never availed myself of the opportunity to ask questions or to even know what was involved in the life of a preacher's wife.

When I met my husband, he was already a preacher. He had been preaching since he was eighteen. We were actually introduced in the same church where he was the second assistant pastor. According to my husband, he knew instantly that I would be his wife. But I "friend-zoned" him, and we remained friends for over six years. It wasn't until after those six years that God opened my eyes to realize that this man was the one He had assigned and ordained for my life. I recognized that I was the one who was really running away from this lifestyle — the life of a preacher's wife. Why? Maybe because I simply was not sure what I was getting myself into or maybe because I was afraid. More than likely, I was probably afraid due to many years in a

ALL THE PREACHER'S WIVES
A Peek Behind The Curtain Of Being A Preacher's Wife

church setting, I would hear so many different stories about the life of a preacher's wife, and I intentionally decided that I did not want that kind of pressure in my life.

A few days after our honeymoon, my husband was invited to preach at a church, which eventually called him as pastor. I thought that we would have a little more time together before I had to share him with other people. I was wrong. Not only were we still trying to get to know each other, but we were also trying to figure out the life of a married couple. Having a successful marriage is already difficult for any couple, but when the office of pastor became part of the dynamic, "fiery darts" from every angle were hurled our way. I definitely was NOT ready for what was about to happen.

Reality Point of View

I already had a strong relationship with God — or so I thought. The life of a preacher's wife opened my eyes to a myriad of things I never imagined facing in life. Oftentimes, as women, we try our best to be there for everyone, and it is in this area of "being there" for others we find ourselves in some sort of chaotic whirlwind that dominates our lives. And truthfully, we do not even recognize it is happening until we have to deal with the residue and debris. I really wish I had learned more about what to expect being a preacher's wife, but I made the mistake of not becoming close to other preachers' wives before I was married. Maybe I could have saved myself from many mistakes.

People tend to have these preconceived notions that preachers' wives have it all together; preachers' wives think they are better than anyone else; preacher's wives this and preachers' wives that. Well, I cannot speak for another preacher's wife, but I am a witness that as a preacher's wife, a mother, a sister, and a friend, I do not have it all together. If there is one thing about being a preacher's wife that I have come to know, it is this: No matter what happens in our lives, God is the head and He comes first. If I can help and encourage anyone who reads my story, my advice would be to never take your eyes off God and His divine plan for your life. As preachers' wives, we are compelled to be on the wall to intercede for every person God places in our lives. We are to be there for our husbands and be their helpers in everything they will face.

For every person reading this book, we are merely vessels of God designed to be used in whatever capacity He sees fit. We all are to be used by God for His glory. Yes, we can always point out other people and their mistakes and even our own disappointments, but if we take our eyes off of the Creator, it will be extremely difficult to continue in our walk with Christ. A preacher's wife's life seems to be more difficult than others because the spotlight is always on the preacher, his wife, and his family. The Bible teaches, "...*For unto whomsoever much is given, of him shall be much required: and to whom men have committed much, of him, they will ask the more.*" The main difference between the woman who is married and the woman who is married to a preacher is...wait for it...wait for it...wait for it...THERE IS NO DIFFERENCE. If we all follow the direct instructions of God's word, He will guide us in EVERY situation, regardless of where we are and who we are in this life.

Psalm 23 — A Preacher's Wife's Declaration

Psalm 23, the Shepherd's psalm, helped me come into alignment with my calling of being a preacher's wife. As Christians, we are all familiar with this memorable passage of scripture. Although I have quoted this passage many times in my life, this psalm truly became and still is an outline and guide for me in my role as a preacher's wife. There are many eye-opening events that occurred in my life, which I will not be able to list in this segment, and I believe the simple, yet profound principles of Psalm 23 will benefit, comfort, and encourage the next woman in her journey of becoming or being a preacher's wife.

1. The LORD is my shepherd; I shall not want.

ALL THE PREACHER'S WIVES
A Peek Behind The Curtain Of Being A Preacher's Wife

God reveals Himself as a Shepherd. And it is this revelation that emphasizes that in God's providence, power, and purpose, He called us believers —as individuals and the church — to do His work. God allows us many opportunities throughout our lifetime to teach others. Therefore, in order for others to be led in the right direction, there must be an individual whom God uses to fulfill His purposes for mankind — a shepherd. The basic definition of a shepherd is someone who watches over a flock to guard, guide, and protect those who are assigned to them. Even though shepherding a group of people can be complex, at the same time, it is much more rewarding knowing you are fulfilling the will of God. A church needs a sound, practical philosophy for Christian leadership based on the Word of God, and a shepherd has the ability to undertake such an assignment.

As a preacher's wife, I had to finally recognize that God is the head of my life, He has preeminence in my life, but He also gave me a shepherd, who is my husband whom I can go to and lean on in every situation. You would think that I would have known this. But the truth of the matter is that many times we say one thing and do another. We believe one thing, yet our lives attest to something totally different. Of course, our husbands have their roles and directions for which they have to seek God for themselves. However, as a preacher's wife, it is my responsibility to follow where my shepherd leads me. I have to trust that my shepherd will guide and lead me where I need to go and keep me safe at all times. I have to realize that my shepherd only wants what is best for me and he will not intentionally cause me to walk blindly into danger. So, know that we have to place God first and trust Him foremost. Then we must know that He placed the shepherd over, and in, our lives for us to help him. The sheep does not only need the shepherd, but the shepherd needs the sheep as well.

Further, as preachers' wives, we are made to help our husbands as they lead God's people. Remember, we are one. We come as a team package to do the will of God. Sometimes, we forget that we are to help our husbands and not hinder or hold them back. *"And the Lord*

ALL THE PREACHER'S WIVES
A Peek Behind The Curtain Of Being A Preacher's Wife

God said, It is not good that the man should be alone; I will make him an help meet for him." It is basically our position as preachers' wives to push our husbands forward and not pull them backwards. We cannot expect to have a successful life as a preacher's wife if we do not adhere to the directions and instructions of the shepherd God has placed over us. The Bible states, *"My sheep hear my voice, and I know them, and they follow me: And I give unto them eternal life; and they shall never perish, neither shall any man pluck them out of my hand."*

2. He maketh me to lie down in green pastures: he leadeth me beside the still waters.

Sheep have a tendency to wander from the herd and get lost. This also is an unfortunate characteristic of Christians. The Bible states, *"We all, like sheep, have gone astray, each of us has turned to his own way."* Because of Christians' similarity to sheep, the people of God need the guidance of a shepherd; consequently, God reveals Himself to us so that we may follow in His footsteps. In modern-day terms, God is our navigation system. Although there are many ways to get to a destination, God guides and directs us on the best path for our lives.

Preachers' wives can concur with this passage of scripture because we look to the Great Shepherd for everything and He directs His under-shepherd (our husbands) to provide a steady, secure, and safe living space ("He maketh me to lie down in green pastures"), as well as steer us in a path of virtue while discovering spiritual order for our lives ("he leadeth me beside the still waters"). The still waters refer to the different seasons in our lives. There are both good seasons and not-so-good seasons; nonetheless, a preacher's wife learns to rely on the rest and refreshment of the "still waters" that only God gives to assist her husband through any storm that arises.

One of the hardest things for women, in general, is to submit to what we cannot control. It is in our nature to want to either know everything, to be in control, or to live in our feelings. Any one of these features can be an undesirable attribute for a preacher's wife. We are human, yes, but we are on a unique journey in a unique position to help others. If we do nothing else to help our husbands, we must learn to listen more, be humble, and not be selfish or quickly offended. I must confess that I had to learn all three of these lessons, and I am still learning them today. When we learn to be honest with each other and ourselves, it becomes a little easier for us to acknowledge, repent, learn from our mistakes, and try again. These kinds of lessons will enhance our spiritual growth and develop within us the desire to do good and to love others as the Bible requires.

3. He restoreth my soul: he leadeth me in the paths of righteousness for his name's sake.

"And the Lord God formed man of the dust of the ground, and breathed into his nostrils the breath of life, and man became a living soul." Are you merely existing? Each breath we take is a representation that God is not through with us yet. We are to walk in His holiness, in His strength, in His truth and righteousness. Simply existing in the presence of God is our ultimate goal as a preacher's wife. We are doing ourselves an injustice when we do not adhere to God's Holy Word and have a special relationship with Him. His Word is true, His word is righteous.

Allowing God to lead us into His righteousness enables every preacher's wife to become more sensitive to the voice of God. Our husbands need a wife by their side to help restore their soul. There is nothing more invigorating for a husband to experience than to have his soulmate breathe life into his soul through the spoken words of God and encouragement on a daily basis. This is why it is important to *not* be self-centered and display a controlling nature. As preachers' wives, we must be able to discern complex issues that invade our lives. God created us to have a special capacity for compassion and understanding that empowers us to build up areas in our husbands' lives that may be lacking. Wives, our husbands are depending on us, and they will listen to us when we are truly connected to God and His word.

4. Yea, though I walk through the valley of the shadow of death, I will fear no evil: for thou art with me; thy rod and thy staff they comfort me.

This scripture identifies how we as preachers' wives cannot allow fear to destroy our call to our husbands. Although we may not always know how to handle a situation (and some situations can be extremely difficult), allowing fear into our lives will only preclude the assignments God has prepared. We know the word declares: *"For God hath not given us the spirit of fear; but of power, and of love, and of a sound mind."* God chooses to use preachers' wives simply because we are the ones most suited to minister to not only our husbands, children, and family, but also to every person God has placed in our circle of influence.

We all know the story of Noah in the Bible. In Noah's case, faith was the first principle. *"By faith Noah, when warned about things not yet seen, in holy fear built an ark to save his family. By his faith, he condemned the world and became heir of the righteousness that comes by faith."* Remember, Noah first believed in God in his ordinary life. Before the test came and before he received the assignment from God, Noah believed in God. And that belief in God—Noah's unshakeable faith—produced his obedience despite any fears he may have faced. Because of his faith, Noah obeyed God's word! We must be like Noah. Sincere faith in God takes God at His word whether that word is joyous or distressing, sensible or senseless, easy or difficult. Preachers' wives are inevitably faced with many valley experiences, but planted in God's word, we are overcomers. We cannot do anything of ourselves, but we can do all things through Christ which strengthens us.

5. Thou preparest a table before me in the presence of mine enemies: thou anointest my head with oil; my cup runneth over.

God does not do anything by happenstance. He is a God of strategic planning and manifestation. God is not a man that He should lie. He keeps His covenant with us, and we must remain obedient to

His word. Why should we expect God to do something for us if we do not trust Him enough to simply follow in His footsteps and honor Him? We all want the benefits from God; however, we seem to forget that we too have a part to play before our cup runs over with blessings. God's word prepares the way that we should go, and our obedience to His word is the impetus for the oil to flow from our heads down to our feet.

Our mission as a preacher's wife is to set the tone for how our blessings emerge in our lives. This tone is called obedience. Do you realize that many times we can hinder what God wants to do exclusively in our lives due to our disobedience? We have to make so many sacrifices as a preacher's wife and oftentimes it gets overwhelming. However, sacrifice is a noble thing. As a matter of fact, Jesus Christ is our ultimate example of what it means to live a sacrificial life. So, our greatest sacrifice is our obedience to God's word and His commands. David said this in Psalm 51:16-17: "*For thou desirest not sacrifice; else would I give it: thou delightest not in burnt offering. The sacrifices of God are a broken spirit: a broken and a contrite heart, O God, thou wilt not despise.*" Many times, we must be broken in order for God to use us in the way He wants to use us. And the majority of the time, He uses us in ways that are not comfortable or easy. No, being a preacher's wife is not always easy, but when we truly align our faith and obedience with God's plans for our lives, He compensates His children with life-balance encounters of His overflowing love.

6.
Surely goodness and mercy shall follow me all the days of my life: and I will dwell in the house of the Lord for ever.

The last tool to encourage those who are preachers' wives or those who may become a preacher's wife is summed up into one very unique word: Grace. Grace gives us the perspective and patience that all preacher's wives should have, desire, and use with every person God brings into their lives. Grace is the primary attribute every preacher's wife should have and develop. Remember, we grow in grace. Every preacher's wife has her own unique story, and you will never know how your story will unfold until you are going through it. Many people look at us from the outside, and they do not see what is really in our hearts. Only God knows our heart.

Unfortunately, preachers' wives usually get a great deal of negative feedback from the people surrounding us. Furthermore, we are even known to demonstrate the frustrations and displeasures in our lives. However, there are many people who sincerely pray for and are devoted to the preacher's wife. God has placed them in our lives for good, and they are there to assist us when we need a shoulder to lean on. Each person who is used by God to assist the ministry as a whole is an anointed vessel, and we are extremely grateful for your sincere love for Christ and your willingness to be used by God to minister to the First Ladies in your lives. Nevertheless, we are constantly in the spotlight in some form or fashion, but through it all, "*...we are more than conquerors through Him that loved us.*"

Final Resolution

People may believe that being a preacher's wife is a proverbial thorn in our flesh because of everything we go through. The word "thorn" communicates the idea of pain, trouble, sufferings, or physical infirmities but not necessarily sin. As a preacher's wife, we absolutely go through many things; however, we cannot consider everything we go through as a thorn. We have to always look at our life from a different perspective, a positive perspective because our life is basically designed for our development into God's plans for our lives. Sometimes God puts "thorns" in our lives because He wants us to trust in Him. Jesus gave us a word about thorns. He said, *"These things I have spoken unto you, that in me ye might have peace. In the world ye shall have tribulation: but be of good cheer; I have overcome the world."* What He meant by that is this: He may not choose to deliver you from the trials you face in this world, but He will never leave you nor will He forsake you as you go through those trials. This is an affirmation of His goodness and mercy that will follow us all the days of our lives. When the time is right, God will miraculously deliver you and grant you His grace to show forth His glory. And those "thorns" serve as reminders that

ALL THE PREACHER'S WIVES
A Peek Behind The Curtain Of Being A Preacher's Wife

when we put our confidence in this corrupt flesh alone, we are destined for failure. So, you can actually consider your thorn in the flesh divine assistance. That's just what grace is: unmerited divine assistance. Jesus told Paul, *"My grace is sufficient for you."*

    To all preacher's wives, we are a divine assistance for our husbands. Because Christ's grace is the instrument by which He gives us whatever we need to get through a trial, to resist a temptation, or to conquer an obstacle. Just as when we are poor, Christ gives us riches, when we are weak, He gives us His power. Just as God forgives us of sin as a result of His grace, He also empowers us to live holy before Him through that same grace. In fact, everything we need to succeed in our walk with Christ comes from God's grace. As preacher's wives, we should all walk in that same grace with the people in our lives. Through good times, and through bad, as women of God, we were equipped to handle anything that comes our way. Wives, and all women of God, whatever you go through, remind yourself that God is with you in every step you take: 1) Trust Him at all times and remain in His presence; 2) be the best wife and mother to your family; and 3) be the best confidante and friend to the people God places in your life. You may ask how we are able to accomplish these important assignments. We are able to achieve these obligations if we "... *seek ye first the kingdom of God, and his righteousness; and all these things shall be added unto you.*" With God's instructions applied, let us…KEEP PUSHING. There is more God wants to achieve in our lives, in our homes, in our churches, and in our communities. And God's grace will empower us through it all.

With everlasting love,
TreSonya Madison Durden

ALL THE PREACHER'S WIVES
A Peek Behind The Curtain Of Being A Preacher's Wife

Linda Kornegay

"I attended that one meeting and no more. You see, I learned to bridle my tongue early on. This means to keep the peace. I really had to hold my tongue towards the end of the pastorship."

11
THE UNFORESEEN GIFT: BEING A PASTOR'S WIFE

No Longer A Deacon

January 20, 2002, excitement was in the air. My husband, Roderick who was an ordained Deacon, was to preach his initial sermon today. Oh, my goodness, I had done all I knew to do to present my husband magnificently to God and to the church. It was an unforeseen gift, of the honor to financially make sure Roderick was dressed in the finest we could afford. As a Deacon, I would make sure his suits and shirts were cleaned, pressed, and ready to wear. As a couple, we did accessorize each other often by wearing the same or similar colors. This Sunday for sure we wore our Sunday best for God. I stood with my red hat trimmed in a black and black two-piece skirt suit wearing black sheer stockings and black leather patent pumps to introduce this new Man of God. Let me share some of the introductions.

God bless you and thank you all for your presence here today. Romans 8: verses 28-30 reads "We know that in everything God works for the good of those who love Him. They are the people God called because that was His plan. God knew them before He made the world. And God decided that they would be like His Son. And those He planned to be like His Son, He also called. And those He called, He also made right with Him. And those He made right, He also glorified."

So today, I am honored to introduce and present Deacon Roderick to you. For truly, he is a man sent by God. This young man was chosen by God to be a blessing to others. During his lifetime, he has done just that. As a child, he brought joy and honor to his parents and to his five brothers. As a young man, he blesses others by giving of his time such as coaching, teaching, and singing. As an older man, he has truly been a loving husband to his wife, a great father to his two children, and a role model to many.

Roderick attended and earned a BS degree from St. Augustine's University along with being one of the founders and singer of an acapella group now known as Style. (Style is currently producing a documentary, expounding on their 40 years of singing.) Singing is truly a gift that Rod has. He sings with several choirs at our church and currently directs the Male choir. You may have been blessed by his singing and musical talents, but Roderick has been a blessing for the Lord in other areas such as a faithful member, a trustee, and a deacon of our church. Now God has a new calling.

My brothers and sisters of Christ, please receive your blessing today for God has chosen a special man to accept the calling into the ministry. A man who has repented, who is obedient, determined, and eager to serve God. A man who is intelligent and committed enough to serve the kingdom of God. He is my mentor, my friend, my husband, and the father of our children. After the song, Deacon Roderick will bless you with his initial sermon from God.

What an honor it is to tell the world a new Minister was in town. Roderick stepped out to preach the Gospel, he looked so handsome to me in his black suit with his red tie. As my husband Deacon Roderick approached the pulpit, I sat at the altar at his feet in a folded chair for the church was packed with people from everywhere.

They had come to witness this man step out and serve God even more. No longer serving as a Deacon but now a Minister.

I admired him, my man Rod a gift from God. To this day and every day, I thank God for Rod. Rod had saved me twice. In my book Daddy Tears, A Daughter's Search found on Amazon, I share how Rod saved me twice in the book. However, I must say hearing the word of God from Rod is the best save, salvation.

Fondly as I remember my journey of becoming a Pastor's wife, memories are rekindled about my husband. I am in awe and amazed. God allowed me to be an unforeseen gift to him again. First, I am his wife and the mother of his two sons. Now I am honored to take care of one of God's chosen ones, who accepted the call of ministry. God gifted me to take care of the Man of God named Rod. It was an exciting and humbling experience as I traveled with my husband teaching, preaching, and evangelizing the gospel of Jesus for three years.

The Recommendation

One day a very dear friend, who happens to be a Pastor, called Rod. He said "listen, down east they are looking for a pastor for one of the churches. I was asked if I knew of anyone to pastor the church. Without hesitation our pastor friend said, I told them Reverend Kornegay. I recommend Reverend Kornegay to be the pastor." After the phone call, Rod informed me, of the recommendation to become a pastor of a church. What, wow, you a pastor I replied. Rod and I laughed lovingly as we were amazed at the honor of God using him. Our pastor friend had recommended Rod and the head deacon of the church wanted to meet him.

It was Thanksgiving 2004 and we traveled to be with our families. We had a feast of food to devour. Our families were together eating, laughing, and just enjoying each other. Rod usually would organize and play sock flag football with the Kornegay teams. Not only were the guys playing but some of the girls played, myself included. Ok,

ALL THE PREACHER'S WIVES
A Peek Behind The Curtain Of Being A Preacher's Wife

I mostly ran out of the way. (smile) However this year the play was changed, a fumble in the game. Rod and Linda did not participate. We shared a touchdown announcement. Rod informed our families he had been recommended to be a pastor. We have an appointment today to meet the Chairman of the Deacon Board. Yes, it is Thanksgiving, and we are going to meet with the Head Deacon. What a great way to show and give thanks, interviewing to be a pastor for God. Before leaving, our family prayed with and for us.

Rod and I were grateful and thankful as we traveled the country roads enjoying the scenery. We arrived at the home of one the sweetest couples we had ever met. An unforeseen gift was truly this couple. They embraced us not with just handshakes, but with hugs, love, and beautiful warm smiles. The home was filled with love and delicious food. The four of us conversed and ate dessert together. Then Deacon and Rod, who had the same birthday, excused themselves to talk in private.

After they talked, we traveled to see the church. Wow! It was a beautiful small white church filled with royal blue carpet. It was breathtaking as the sun shined thru the colored stained-glass windows. Look where God wanted to place us, an unforeseen gift, His church. The tour of the church ended. The Deacon informed other candidates for Pastor had come to preach and meet the congregation. With the most handsome smile, the Deacon looked at his beautiful wife and then back at Rod and I and asked a question. Will you come and preach 2nd Sunday in December? You have been highly recommended Reverend Kornegay. My wife and I are pleased but the Deacon stated the people need to meet you. Rod smiled and said yes sir, I will be honored to come. My heart filled with gratitude as Rod and I started a new journey of love, God's love.

Sunday, December 12, 2004, had arrived to meet the waiting congregation. We woke up early to prepare for our trip. Of course, clothes had been laid out and ready to put on the night before. Wait a minute, I was like should I wear this dress or that one? Rod was like whatever you wear, you will look beautiful. Linda, baby, I need you to get dressed so we can leave on time. I do not want to be late. First impressions can make or break you. (One nugget I will share that I learned is to try not to delay the man of God, you may get left.)

Yes, a trip, it was almost 3 hours we had to travel to reach the church. We were on our way dressed in royal blue. Although the trip was not just around the corner, we were totally excited about going to church. We arrived and were greeted by one of the most beautiful loving fiery spirited ministers. Sunday school was still in attendance, so we joined in quietly. After Sunday School, we were introduced to the other ministerial staff. The Chairman of the Deacon board was there to greet us and introduced us to many of the wonderful unforgettable loving people of the church and community. It was an amazing Sunday. Roderick preached the word. He was invited back two more 2nd Sundays before being informed he would be their new pastor.

The Words of Wisdom for First Lady

My husband was now the Pastor, and I am now called First Lady. To be the First Lady is more than a name. Therefore, I wanted to be the best I could be. First and foremost, I knew I would still seek after God's heart. As a Deaconess, I was taught to serve and now being a graduate to First Lady, it was automatic to continue to serve. However, I needed wisdom and knowledge. I asked questions of my former First Lady of 28 years at our home church. Now she does not want to be called First Lady but just her name. She is truly a down-to-earth woman of God who keeps it real. I love my former and current First Lady. They are both loving ladies.

One piece of advice among many my First Lady of 28 years told me along with my former Pastor was, "Now Linda, you were not called to pastor. You are not a member of that church so do not attend the church meetings." I did attend one meeting but I should have listened to my First Lady.

ALL THE PREACHER'S WIVES
A Peek Behind The Curtain Of Being A Preacher's Wife

At church meetings, you hear some people talking and you know they are Christians, but their talk is not always Christian-like. They will talk to or at each other and even the Pastor as if they had lost their minds. I attended that one meeting and no more. You see, I learned to bridle my tongue early on this means to keep the peace. I really had to hold my tongue towards the end of the pastoral ship. You must keep the peace: peace for your mental health, peace for your husband, peace for your home, and peace so it will quietly overflow into the church. Not just peace for the church building but for you, you are the church. Peace is needed and good to keep. Even though some meetings are heated, they would usually always hold hands and pray. Now really hold hands after you have told my husband or others off, God has a sense of humor. God is totally in control for He was still in the midst. The people knew to pray. Prayer is always appropriate mad or not. Pray because God can and will shift the atmosphere in His time. Don't stop praying but I will say don't pray a long prayer but keep it short. You don't want to be known as a lying prayer warrior.

I had the pleasure of receiving advice from one of the sweetest Women of God, I have ever met. Her husband was a pastor for 50 years and she was a virtual First Lady for 50 years plus. To be in her presence, you felt God. You respected her. You loved her. She loved you. She loved her church. She told me to always respect my husband. Do not criticize him in public. When it is you need to talk with your husband about a disagreement, do so in private. You are the only one to remind him, God chose him in the midnight hour. During the midnight hour is the hardest time when your husband may need you. You are the only one that knows how to make him feel special. Honor your husband. Love your husband and let the church know and see you love him. This first lady of fifty-plus years reminded me to love the church. Love the people. They want to love and need love and you will need and want love also. Show love, Linda this is easy for you. You show and give love genuinely and the people will feel it. Even though you show love, you will feel hurt sometimes. This is when you pray, and you can go to the person in the spirit of love and privately discuss the misunderstanding. Only go if you are led by God and not yourself.

ALL THE PREACHER'S WIVES
A Peek Behind The Curtain Of Being A Preacher's Wife

Remember God fights all battles, and all battles are not yours to fight. Sometimes, you will have to be quiet. (Remember to keep the peace.)

My former pastor of 28 years, whom I loved dearly also gave me advice. And yes, I do love my current pastor as well. However, my previous pastor of 28 years told me to be me. He said you will encounter people who may be jealous of you. My Linda, you still be you. You dress nice and you carry yourself in a respectable manner. You look nice, just be nice.

Linda, you assist your husband and prop him up when he feels low. Encourage his heart. You are the best cheerleader for him. Let him hear you say Amen. He needs to hear your words of encouragement. Your voice may be the only voice of love. Linda, do not show favoritism to the church people. Treat them all the same. Love the people and show them love.

With Love, The Church Family

Love was felt from the beginning in this church family. They are a group of people who smile, hug and nod with love. We found it easy to feel the warmth of love from the congregation and the community. It was in October of 2005 they installed Roderick as pastor. Wow, this was a momentous occasion, the church was overflowed with people. Our home church, visiting churches, family, and friends came to this Christian historical service. The church family had prepared a good old-fashioned country meal, collard greens, fried chicken, potato salad and so much more. The desserts were mouthwatering. The fiery-spirited minister made her special delicious top-secret tea to be served with other beverages. Our home church, family, and friends who attended stated they really felt welcomed. Also, they said we would be alright with this new church family. Love lives here, love was felt here but most importantly God is at this church.

So, there we have it. We are now the Pastor and First Lady of this family country church. Now, let us go to work. Pastor did his

ALL THE PREACHER'S WIVES
A Peek Behind The Curtain Of Being A Preacher's Wife

pastoral duties. I did a few things with his permission on my own. God allowed me to start a Senior Ministry. Oh, my seniors are and were so precious to me. Some would say we are too old to do this or do that. Gently I would remind them, they got up and they can do it. They enjoyed visiting the nursing homes and giving gifts. They are so deserving of the celebratory services we had to recognize them. We loved our seniors. I loved my seniors, and they loved me, they loved us.

The church was growing with a few more children in attendance. I wanted to involve the youth, so I initiated a children's choir, named The Shining Stars. They were my shining stars because of their beautiful smiles, and they were singing for God. They loved singing during our morning worship service. Children are totally a precious gift from God. We had three beautiful singers singing to the glory of God. Sometimes, their big sister would sing with them. An unforeseen gift was the love of those children. May God always bless them and keep them.

Pastor worked tirelessly to involve the church in becoming a better church. Even though small, they did mighty work for our Lord. Under the leadership of my husband, vacation bible school was restarted, and bible study was restarted. He even started a basketball tournament 3 On 3. I was even a coach for the 3-on-3 team since the pastor had to work. The pastor was teaching, preaching, and doing the work of the Lord, so the church could be edified.

This church family loved us. They showed appreciation at the Pastor's anniversary. They even did a First Lady service, one of the loving ministers headed this up. She would often tell me she loves me. An unforeseen gift, God using people to shower us with love. The church family loved me and honored me as their First Lady. However, they would request I sit down even though help was needed. Our church had a small congregation and when we had other churches to come and fellowship, we would often feed. Therefore, I would serve them along with the kitchen staff. They did not particularly like this.

ALL THE PREACHER'S WIVES
A Peek Behind The Curtain Of Being A Preacher's Wife

They would say, "First Lady, you should sit down, you are the First Lady." With love, I informed I too am here to serve. I was told you are a different type of first lady. With love again, I informed I am striving to get into heaven just like you. So often, we worked together, and sometimes, they insisted that I sit, and sometimes I did, with love.

Proud and Honored

I was the First Lady of a church for eleven years and seven months. I was so proud and honored. This was an unforeseen gift being a Pastor's wife. Love was felt. God gave me my loving husband who became pastor. I love my husband. I laughed often with my husband so much so that tears of joy would flow. Sometimes the quiet tears were not of joy, but I had to pull on God. He would remind me of the scriptures to encourage myself. One of my favorites is Joel 2:21: Rejoice and be glad for the Lord has done marvelous things.

One of the most profound things God did was to allow me to marry my husband. He feels my love from me. As I mentioned in a recent interview, I lust for my husband. Meaning longing to be with him, help him, support him, and provide for him. Whatever will make him feel empowered, the lust, the desire was there to please my husband. No one else should have the power to come between us. I am my husband's First Lady twice. We married each other. He is my first and only man and I am his first and only lady. God sealed it publicly twice by way of marriage and by using a small country-loving church to announce to the world, Linda is the First Lady.

God anointed this loving church to be shepherded by us just for a little while. God gave me, First Lady, an extended family, that I had never met, a new church family. I loved this church family. I respected them. I gave my best. I had fun and an awesome fellowship with this church. I worked for this church in love. I was proud and honored to be called their First Lady.

ALL THE PREACHER'S WIVES
A Peek Behind The Curtain Of Being A Preacher's Wife

First Lady Left the Church

The time had come that all the spiritual planting had been done that Pastor was chosen to do. The shift in atmosphere of this loving church had changed. Sometimes whispers of disappointment were spoken by the congregation. Sometimes it was not a whisper but a voice too loud and I chose to no longer hear. It was unwanted conversations and changes occurring. Despair and heartbreak were felt. My husband was relentless to not giving up so easily, but the church body had voted and spoken. My journey as First Lady with this church body was over. I served gallantly with my husband. I served diligently for God. On the 2nd Sunday in November of 2016, I gave my last gifts to the Seniors, who were usually honored during this month. I gave an unforeseen gift of being a Pastor's Wife. I left in love. I left happily knowing God allowed me to be the best I could be. I left knowing I had served God faithfully. Sometimes God closes one door and opens a brand new one. An unforeseen gift this First Lady left the church with joy and love. This First Lady left the way she came together with her husband and God's love.

Ma Lena Evans

"Even in the whispers and secret discussions, they gave us our space but made it clear – they didn't want anything to do with what we were doing."

ALL THE PREACHER'S WIVES
A Peek Behind The Curtain Of Being A Preacher's Wife

12
JUST AS I AM

I never signed up, applied for, or secretly desired the position of First Lady. In fact, I remember saying I did not want to be a pastor's wife because of the expectations and congregational talk you had to endure. Well, needless to say, it is exactly what I became and have been for over 38 years. I have never loved that title, but I do embrace being a woman of God and the attributes and responsibilities according to scripture recorded in Titus 2:3-5 and Proverbs 31.

When my husband became pastor of his initial church in the early 80s, I don't recall the title of First Lady being used as it is so commonly used now. I was just referred to as his wife, the pastor's wife, or what the children would often say, Miss Reverend Evans. Having the title of First Lady is almost like receiving an honorary degree; it is bestowed upon you when you are married to a pastor, and you must wear it with all its rights and privileges, and challenges. You must quickly learn to navigate through spiritual and non-spiritual obstacle courses. You must be committed to on-the-job training from multiple directions, and you must be ready to serve. Whether you recognize it or not, you are under a microscope from every angle. Sometimes you can feel it and at other times you cannot. The people in the congregation will judge everything about you in any given situation. It may be your hair, your make-up or lack thereof, your style of dress, your voice, your ability to speak, and your relationship with your husband and children. They will even evaluate where you sit in church and whom you have conversations with before and after service. The lens on their microscope is powerful and it can be used for or against you, depending on the motive. But remember, you have a microscope too. You are also evaluating others and making judgment calls and decisions about who, what, when, where, and how. You must use the word of God wisely as your offensive and defensive weapon of choice and learn to endure hardness like a good soldier as recorded in 2 Timothy 2:3-5.

"What does it feel like to be a First Lady or the wife of the pastor?" This is a question I have answered numerous times. My answer is simple. First and foremost, you must be a Christian - a follower of Christ. You must have your own personal and motivating relationship with Christ to assist you in being steadfast and unmovable according to I Corinthians 15:58. Without this foundation, you will be wavering and wandering in so many ways.

Before I married my husband, he was not a pastor, but he let me know from the beginning about his aspirations to serve God in pulpit ministry. Our common ground was our love for God and others. Our uncommon ground was our worship experience. He was accustomed to a reserved Christian Church background and my background was more active or Pentecostal/charismatic. During that time in the '70s, we would have been seen as polar opposites; however, we could see God in both settings and respected each other's mode of worship. Even though his setting was more reserved, I could see God moving and speaking through people in a different worship experience and he came to understand the outward display of emotions that were reflected in my church's worship setting. These differences never separated us; they complimented both of us. Today, these lines seem to be erased and we come to worship in spirit and in truth (John 4:24).

The Silent Partner: Just as Mary in the bible pondered things in her heart, I too, have pondered many things in my mind and heart as the wife of a pastor. Some things have been so good and others have been so troubling. It is good to know that a group of believers called your spouse to the pastor or shepherd them. This also means they are accepting the backpack he carries with him and that includes you and any children.

I believe there is a honeymoon period where the church is getting to know their new pastor and his family and he is getting acquainted with them as well. During this time, you have to walk softly and try not to disturb anything that is already in place since you did not put it there. Your primary role at this stage is to look, listen and learn carefully. Notice things that are said, as well as, things that are not said, and take note of who is speaking. Take note also of who is not speaking but carries a voice to be heard. It is during these times that you have to take on a spirit of discernment. I have learned that a seat of power and authority exists within others in the church and you must recognize and respect it. You must know and study people who are godly and those who are only pretending to be. Know who is for your husband and who is against him as pastor. Both of these individuals are noteworthy and have their own following within the church. Use wisdom and discretion when dealing with each and be kind and gentle because a soft answer turns away wrath and harsh words stir up anger. (Proverbs 15:1)

I have observed from other pastors' wives that becoming too vocal at the onset of your husband's pastoral ministry can be a detriment or hindrance to his ministry. One first lady confided in me that her husband lost his church because she talked too much. From this I learned, you can say too much at the wrong time or not enough at the right time. Learning to balance these two takes time, patience, and humility. Being able to control your tongue takes practice and it can be done.

I have had many ideas but could not express them for fear of being too overbearing or overstepping my boundaries. Therefore, I had to learn to filter my ideas through others in order for them to be accepted or rejected. Your spouse does not want it to seem that you are running things and he is not in control. It takes humility to pass your ideas on to others and let them enjoy the credit. In the end, the glory really belongs to God. You are just a vessel. Respect his role and know your goal is not to be in control. Everything you do or say will affect your spouse as pastor and the congregation.

Knowing Who You Are/Protect Your Space: Take time to get to know who you are and what motivates you. Know how far you are willing and able to go with people entering your life and the life of your home. You are responsible for maintaining your home and its atmosphere. Create an environment that is safe for your husband when he needs to retreat from the congregation. Invite others when necessary and always maintain a spirit of hospitality when others are invited. You should pay close attention to your husband's desires and whether he wants a quiet and peaceful atmosphere when he returns home. If you are not an entertainer within your home, consider using another gathering place. You may need to set clear boundaries so that people will not drop by unexpectedly or miss seeing you at home. Know that it is ok to say that you and the family are having dinner or involved in a project with the children. Always offer to get back to them after you are finished. This sends a message that you are protecting your family time and it establishes quality time as being important in your household.

My husband established a date night for us and informed the congregation. It was wonderful to know that he valued and protected his time with me; and, it set a precedent for other men to follow up with their wives.

Church Duties: I like to feel responsible for what I am doing and take ownership of my role. Ask questions and be clear about expectations to avoid unnecessary disagreements. Your role is to help and not to hinder the work of your husband/pastor or the congregation. If and when you do not feel qualified to take on a particular leadership role, please say "no" gently or just "not at this time" is appropriate. You need time to grow and get a feel of the people you are working with at any given time. Sometimes people are testing you and your character and you must be ready to give an answer. If you have young children, their needs will help dictate what you can and cannot do at any given time. It is wise to let your husband know when you are being asked to take on roles. He is an excellent source of knowledge and incites for various positions and what the expectations will be. Sometimes he may want you to take a lesser role in order to grow another person into leadership.

There will be roles that a previous first lady fulfilled that the church wants you to do also. Again, know who you are and what you feel capable of doing with your circumstances. Personally, I have never been confronted with a list of duties for the First Lady. However, there are some unwritten expectations that you may want to follow through with depending on your church body. For instance, some First Ladies may assist with communion, wear gloves and hats on different occasions, and lead worship. Whatever you do, it should be to glorify Christ. Trying to implement or suggest change will sometimes invite opposition or immediate resistance. Even though your idea of change may be valid, the timing may not be right. So, therefore, in all your getting, get understanding as outlined in Proverbs 4:7.

When I learned about "sacred cows" it did not make sense to me. Why would the church want to hold onto ideas or things that hindered progress within the church? The concept of Sacred Cows was explained to me as things people had given to the church that represented their values and/or their ancestors' value to the church and their items should not or could not be removed. If removed, you were removing them and that was not good. These items often included donated books, pictures, furniture, wall hangings, etc. I discovered throughout the years, that in due time, these items took care of themselves. All battles are not meant to be won on the same day. Let the Lord work it out for you.

Alone: There are times I feel alone. Why? The reasons vary. Sometimes there is no one you trust well enough to keep your confidence. Sometimes you just want to vent or let your hair down and then move on without the fear of someone else holding on to something you let go of by the time you hang up the phone. Sometimes, you have to keep your feelings and opinions to yourself. It is during these times that Jesus becomes the comforter and the friend you long for to pour out your soul. Being alone prepares you to recognize who Jesus truly is, and it gives you a testimony of how impactful He really is in your life.

There are times you need to know and experience loneliness to identify with women within your circle and congregation who feel isolated or find it hard to make friends or reach out to others. I discovered speaking to your loneliness will help you maneuver through it. Articulating why and when you feel lonely, where you feel lonely, and who makes you feel this way are all a part of self-talking you can do with yourself. Writing down your answers will help you keep track of your feelings and the duration. Being alone and experiencing loneliness will come and go but it does not need to overstay its visit with you.

Staying in My Lane: I have not been called by God to pastor or co-pastor a church alongside my husband. It was my husband who received the call from God and from a church body of baptized believers to pastor and shepherd their congregation. I support other women as co-pastors who have received such a call from God to do this. As my husband's wife and as a follower of Christ, I am called to share in his ministry and support him. When I attend church and Bible Study regularly, accompany him on preaching engagements, render Christian service to others, teach VBS or Sunday School, and contribute to the financial support of the church, I am supporting the ministry my husband has been called to do. When these things are missing from the pastor's wife, the husband's ministry cannot be as effective as it should be. I recognize him as the priest of our home. I pray for him because I know when he is vulnerable. I lift him up when he has been wounded by the attacks of others. Know what your husband's needs are in ministry. Others may think they know, but you are the one who truly knows. You are his protector from people who constantly pull on him and offer very little in return. Use your hands to anoint him and speak over his life. Include him in your daily prayers and call his name out unto the Lord. Ask God to keep him sane and healed. Thank God for giving him to you. Honor your marriage vows and uphold them.

Settle your disagreements at home. Guard your speech, tone of voice, appearance, and motives when you are in public. Know that you are not perfect, just forgiven by the grace of God. Accept that and continue to move on. There will be another day and new mercies will appear. Be quick to apologize and own up to your misgivings. Never forget that you are being watched. Even the children watch you. Evaluate your conversations and watch what you do. Even when you go grocery shopping, people will recognize you as the pastor's wife or the First Lady of your church. Just keep in mind when you leave your home, you represent more than yourself. I remind myself that I represent Christ as His ambassador. Every time I step out, I represent a group of other women at the church where my husband is the under-shepherd. I want to represent them well in any given setting or situation.

The Titus 2 Woman: Although society seems to support the liberated woman who is free to do as she chooses without the help and support of others, it is contrary to the women in Titus 2. In this scripture, I find support and explicit instructions that have been written to older and younger women. The older women in this scripture are seasoned and mature. They have been groomed and are ready to teach, not preach. They know how to reach others with the word of God. They have been faithful and now they can pass on the fruit of their labor. As wives of pastors, we should be able to teach our younger women how to conduct themselves in church and at home with their spouses and children. We should not be offended when other Godly women approach us about our appearance or demeanor when they have the right motive. They are our stop signs, our red lights or flags on the field to help us re-examine ourselves. But if we ignore all of the warning signs, we may collide with others or cause them to be misled by our failure to listen and take heed to instructions.

I have witnessed that most women will listen and agree with Titus 2, but do not try to implement or apply this scripture without resistance. Most become resentful or just ignore what you are trying to convey. Their resentment can be seen in their tone of voice, their response, their body language, and their eyes. Despite all of this, the Titus 2 woman is embedded in the word of God for a godly reason and the pastor's wife should be among the first to receive godly instructions from other mature women in Christ. We are called to lead and to be examples for the world to see and witness Christ in our everyday lives. For it is in Him we live and in Him, we move and have our being according to Acts 17:28.

Let Us Pray: Our father and our one and only Savior, I pray for our total well-being as women of faith who aspire to be just like you. Give us godly desires and turn our minds away from the world. Set us on the road to spiritual renewal. Let our dim lights be brightened by your holiness in our lives. Allow us to become our sister's keeper. Take the little that we bring today and turn it into so much more for your kingdom and for your glory. Amen.

Merl Johnson

"After twenty-three years, just when I thought I had the hang of my life as a deaconess, something happened. I was utterly surprised, but at the same time, I was fearful and apprehensive."

ALL THE PREACHER'S WIVES
A Peek Behind The Curtain Of Being A Preacher's Wife

13
MOLDING CLAY

"⁴And the vessel that he made of clay was marred in the hand of the potter: so he made it again another vessel, as seemed good to the potter to make it. ⁵Then the word of the Lord came to me, saying, ⁶O house of Israel, cannot I do with you as this potter? saith the LORD. Behold, as the clay is in the potter's hand, so are ye in mine hand, O house of Israel."

Jeremiah 18: 4-6, KJV

God created each of us in His image, with His spirit inside of us. He does not make mistakes, but just like the potter, sometimes He sees something else in us than the original plan. It could be our life experiences that create this alternative picture of who we are, or who we are to be. Just as the potter was able to re-mold his creation into another vessel, God sees fit to sometimes remold us. That is not to say we were flawed in the beginning. It just shows that He has found a different use for the set of skills He has endowed us with. We see this remolding process as growth. It is through growth in God that we are able to truly understand our purpose and to be able to withstand the things we are put through in order to get us to that purpose. The road to get there will not be easy at all, not even for the average person. But that road gets considerably narrower and bumpier for the pastor's wife. Let me explain to you just what I mean.

First, allow me to introduce myself. I am Merl Johnson, a God-fearing woman; a mother of four children; a native of Philadelphia,

ALL THE PREACHER'S WIVES
A Peek Behind The Curtain Of Being A Preacher's Wife

Mississippi; and a down-home country girl. I married at the age of eighteen. I have worked in supervisory positions for most of my career. I retired as a Property/Laundry Supervisor at a prison facility. As you can see, I have had quite a life interacting with people on a daily basis. Sometimes it was favorable, sometimes unfavorable; but each interaction helped me to grow as an individual. Each moment of growth helped me to become that which the potter intended for me, but that is the history of my secular life, who I was outside of the church. What do you mean by secular history?

Let me tell you about my walk in the ministry. I have lived my life as a pastor's wife for twenty-two years, although I feel as if it has been forty-five years. My husband was a deacon in the Baptist church for twenty-three years. He was very devoted to the ministry, even as a deacon. I also took my role as a deaconess very seriously. And because I took it so seriously, a great commitment was required. I was never the deaconess who felt it was okay to let my hair down. I took on the church persona wherever I went. This meant there were things I would previously partake in, such as parties or gatherings of friends, that I now veered away from. I didn't know what it would look like for me, a deaconess, to be involved in that kind of lifestyle. I was a representation of my church and my husband. As a deaconess, there is certainly a standard of responsibility you should meet. This responsibility is not just your husband alone. You are the supporter of the footstool of the church. The deacon has great accountability in his role in the church. They help to carry on the mission of God, and how that looks specifically with the pastor. As a deaconess, your responsibilities are just as important. Not only are you concerned with supporting your husband, but you are also charged with supporting the pastor's wife. Her needs (as they relate to the church) are of high concern for you because she is the often-overlooked member of the ministry. Most congregations are in tune with the needs of the pastor; making sure he has a certain robe, making sure he has his beverage of choice in the pulpit, making sure he is comfortable enough to preach the Word, but also making sure he knew they loved and supported him. For the pastor's wife, she may also need some refreshments. She may have had

ALL THE PREACHER'S WIVES
A Peek Behind The Curtain Of Being A Preacher's Wife

a rip in her hem and needed a quick fix before service started. She may have a fussy child that takes her focus from the pastor during the service. It was my role as the deaconess to see what needs the pastor's wife may have and help to alleviate them. I learned more about this as I became the pastor's wife. As a deaconess, you are also a role model for other young ladies in your church. I learned very early that your walk is more important than your talk. Young ladies are watching everything you say and do. If your actions do not align with your words, this will be a stumbling block in their religious journey. They may not understand why you told them one thing but did another. So, I had to make sure that I practiced what I said because they had no problem asking for clarity on those issues. This is why I said it felt like forty-five years in the ministry. I was there with my husband at prayer services, church services, and meeting the needs of people in the community. As deaconesses and pastors' wives, we are not just sideline cheerleaders. We are more like the backup athletes on the team.

After twenty-three years, just when I thought I had the hang of my life as a deaconess, something happened. I was utterly surprised, but at the same time, I was fearful and apprehensive. My life totally changed. I became the Pastor's Wife. I had no idea what to expect because there was no welcoming committee of preachers' wives gathered to show me the ropes. I had become confident in my supporting role of deaconess, but what was this new position going to require? Little did I know that God was preparing me in those twenty-three years as a deaconess, but that was just the groundwork. Things would be utterly different. Now I faced even more responsibility. God equips us with the basic information we need to build a strong foundation for our lives. God intended for our unresolved hurts, challenges, and abuses to lead us to new experiences of spiritual growth to make us strong and show us how to extend the love He has shown us to others. He wants to mold us into the women we should be.

One of the most important things I found out about becoming a *First Lady* of the church did not come as a word of advice given by wise counsel. This revelation came through me living life the best way

ALL THE PREACHER'S WIVES
A Peek Behind The Curtain Of Being A Preacher's Wife

I knew how. ***Be yourself;* don't try to imitate someone else.** God made you to be you, not anyone else. Initially, this was not easy for me. I wanted to have someone I could pattern what I would do after, a pastor's wife role model. I thought, at first, if I could sing like other ministers' wives, oh, that would be awesome (that didn't happen). God had me to know I must seek the guidance of the Holy Spirit to be a role model for other women. He had to show me that I could blend with other women in amplifying Jesus Christ while never losing my individuality. You stay in your place and position as a minister's wife. Being a role model for other women is not a performance. We are not role-playing in a play but responding to life off-stage and out of the glare of the lights. Our lives are on display; therefore, we must be careful what we present. We are Christians, first and foremost. The label of being Christian means that you should live Christ-like. Oftentimes, we find ourselves being contested and opposed by the very people we are leading. Even as the *First Lady* of a church, I have been challenged by members in our congregation many times. Some may do it to solidify their importance in the role of the church. Some people want to try to see how much the pastor's wife knows. Just remember, God placed you there in that position and He will give you what you need when you need it.

There will be some people who will befriend you just to get information. Yes, this happens in the church too. Let me advise you, to be mindful of the conversations you have with people in your congregation. Sometimes it's what you don't say that means so much to the wrong individual. Don't discuss your and your husband's business with his church members. We are humans. We have disagreements. We learned how to get through them. We learned to value each other's thoughts and feelings. We recognized the importance of communication, and we vowed to never let the sun set on our anger. We realized that sacrifice was not a one-way street, and that we both move harmoniously. Because of our love and concern for one another, it is really not a sacrifice to us, it is an opportunity to enhance the lives of our significant other. Members of the congregation many times put the pastor on a high pedestal, thinking he should make no mistakes. Those same members would not understand the human errors involved in being a part of this ministry. That is why I say don't discuss your private life with church members. Learn how to communicate effectively with your husband to lessen the number of disagreements, or just allow those disagreements to be the stepping stones to a better understanding of your spouse. You must remember, he is your spouse, and you are still blending two lives as one. Those differences that other couples have, you may find them arising in your marriage as well. The difference can be your understanding of the Word and how God can guide you through those times. Your lives are being molded as an example for other couples within the congregation.

    I have heard people say, "don't show favoritism, treat them all the same." I don't show favoritism. I treat them all right, but I can't treat them all the same. They are different. You have some that show no love. You have some that show much genuine love. You can't have a universal method of dealing with the congregation. What may work with some will not work with others. You should let them know how much you appreciate them for caring. Ask God for discernment in how to treat each of them. Remember that your goal in the ministry is to win souls for Christ, not make the most friends out of the members. Keep the focus on His ministry. He may be molding some people out of your lives for a reason.

    Most everyone in the church is watching the pastor's wife. We are a representation of the pastor at all times. People want to see how we react to things and people in the church and the community. As a pastor's wife dealing with women in the church, discord will sometimes occur. Prayer and yielding to the Lord is my strength. I asked the Lord for help with guidance, leadership, and wisdom. I do not take sides in disputes. If I make comments (which I rarely do), I do not make any comments before checking the facts, even when words are peacemaking. Let people sort out their problems themselves, with the help of God. I can pray on their behalf, for God to take away the confusion, but I don't lend my thoughts to the conversation.

ALL THE PREACHER'S WIVES
A Peek Behind The Curtain Of Being A Preacher's Wife

Remember, what you say may be reversed and may be released as a rumor. I do not take part in the clique in the church.

As God is molding you into the pastor's wife you will see some major changes happen in your life. My friends are fewer now. Though in the beginning I did not understand why this was so, I don't really miss those friends I had before I became a pastor's wife. God has replaced that time and space with other things that lead to kingdom building. Satan is always present. He will cause you to have a pity party with yourself. You begin to think "Now I can't go to this event, can't go to the movie, can't go to the family reunion, ball games and other social events because of a church event." Then others may ask "why do you have to be at the church all the time? You miss out on all the fun." Sometimes, God may be protecting you from some detrimental behaviors at those events. If it is truly something you wish to attend and does not work against the mission of God, all it takes is scheduling. Family is important. I had to learn that there is a life outside of the church walls. I thought I had to be at the building every time the doors were opened. God had me realize that spending time with family was important too. Those Godly friends you have will understand this and will be supportive, not critical of your time.

In this new role, I had to understand the significance of time management. Spending time with your husband is crucial. He has family and church problems to deal with. He needs a shoulder to lean (or cry) on. Just saying, "Honey, I love you" can mean so much. I am that shoulder. Sure, there were times I needed a shoulder. He was busy with church business. That's when Satan tried to enter the mind. I had to be strong. I prayed to God to give me the strength I needed at that time. It didn't happen in fifteen minutes, but it did happen. In the meantime, I did not confide in another church or community member, because not everyone will be understanding. Some may use that information to come between you and your husband, spreading false business against him. Therefore, I turned to Him. He is the Potter and sometimes, as the songwriter says, "just a little talk with Jesus makes it right." Had I confided in someone else may have started a rumor to undermine his ministry. Being a pastor's wife, feel assured that most women (and some men) are watching. Make sure you are displaying what you want them to see.

Isn't it true that, when it comes to people, we very often judge a book by its cover? People scrutinize our outward appearance and draw conclusions about our inward qualities. Whether it is right or wrong isn't really a question, it's simply a fact of life. While the Lord looks at the heart for the inward qualities, most everyone else looks at the outward appearance. (1 Samuel 16:7). So, is it wrong for Christian women to want to be beautiful and attractive? No, it's not, as long as we desire to be beautiful in a modest way. First of all, we are the wife of the pastor. We do not want to represent him by looking anything less than our best. In the congregation's eyes, it will speak to his ministry. Secondly, we want to appeal to our spouse, not have them longing for us to look more presentable. We are humans and have desires. One of our emotional desires is to be desired and to have a significant other who is desirable. You do not realize how much easier it is for the pastor to complete his mission when he knows he has home on point. One of our goals is to demonstrate God's goodness in our lives. We can't look like we are in a bad predicament and expect others to want to live a life for Him. Nonetheless, to be real with this, there is some attire a pastor's wife should not wear. First Timothy 2:9 says, *"In like manner also that women adorn themselves in modest apparel."* Our appearance should reflect something about our relationship with God. Our appearance also reveals something about our attitude. We should not dress for attention or prestige. Instead our apparel should indicate that God provides and that worshiping Him will bring blessings. Yet, it should not draw ungodly attention. Our mission is to remind others of Him, not the length of our hem.

Even with the responsibilities of the ministry, it is a blessing, not a curse. Be thankful God has chosen your husband to lead His people. It is an honor bestowed on those He feels He can trust. Your spouse has quite an important role. But don't get it twisted, your role is equally important. You are his helpmate. You are to aid your husband

ALL THE PREACHER'S WIVES
A Peek Behind The Curtain Of Being A Preacher's Wife

in whichever way you can. This aid can come in many different formats. As I have stated before, all congregations are different. Some welcome the pastor's wife to be a part of the events. Some do not. Do not allow this to get in your way of being that helpmate your spouse needs. If you are not part of the church's events in a leadership way, that's ok. Maybe God is protecting you from some added drama you may not need in your life. Remember there's enough for you to do, taking care of your husband and family. Focus on what He is molding you for. The rest will take care of itself.

One of the most important lessons I learned as a pastor's wife is to take care of number one. Yes, you are a helpmate for your spouse, but what kind of help can you be if you are worn down yourself? When taking care of needs, make sure you don't leave yourself out. You always need some me time. One of the hardest things for me was going to business meetings with my husband. We've always been very close to each other. He had to sit up front. I would always sit somewhere alone. I did not want to sit beside any of the members because I felt it may influence their voting decision. I prayed about it. God gave me peace of mind. I placed my desire to sit next to my husband to show support aside. I would go to the meeting and have me a book to read or I would consume my time with writing. The important thing was, I was there for his support. Fortunately, I was able to go with him almost every time. There were no children at home. He accepted his calling the year my youngest daughter graduated from high school, so there were no small children that would require a large portion of my time.

My husband told me he promised God if He would spare my life, that he would do whatever God asked of him. I had a serious illness as a younger adult woman. In 1979, when my youngest child was three months old, I was diagnosed with Crohn's Disease. This diagnosis was preceded by months of tests and medical probes. I had a young doctor, and I was his sixteenth patient. He promised me that he would find the reason for my suffering. After weeks of tests, I prayed one night that God would let him find what was wrong with me. The next morning the doctor came in and told me my diagnosis. I knew it was God! But this was only the beginning. I suffered for several years. I had two colectomies (removal of portions of my colon), followed by fifteen years of taking steroids (nineteen pills daily) just to live. My doctor told me that I would have to continue taking steroids and get on disability, but I prayed to God, and against the doctor's orders, I laid the pills down, went back to work, and asked God to show me what he wanted me to do. God answered our prayers. Thirty years in remission from Crohn's! Hallelujah! Today, I am still blessed to be here. But as our family grew older, we didn't really experience the "empty nest syndrome." God filled it with His ministry. He helped us realize our growth in Him as He continued to mold us.

Being a pastor's wife is truly an honor. I would say overall, it's been good for me. Christianity holds that God sets the standard for what is right, just, beautiful, and good. We are accountable because we are endowed with the capacity to be responsible for the moral consequences of our behaviors. We can't go through life blaming others for what we choose to do. Our consequences are a by-product of our actions. We must choose good over evil, right over wrong. In those instances where we may make the wrong decision, we must hold ourselves accountable, not placing blame where it does not belong. Being a pastor's wife doesn't give me the opportunity to be exempt from living a Godly life. Matthew 12:36 says *But I say unto you, that every idle word that man shall speak, they shall give account thereof in the day of judgment* (KJV). As ministry leaders, pastors and their wives need to surrender their lives to Christ by saying, Lord, you made me while I was in my mother's womb. You know me completely (reference to Psalm 139: 13-16). Lord, you bought me with your blood. You paid the price for me. I no longer belong to myself. You have the right to direct my life. Therefore, our tongue should reflect the power of His Word. No utterance coming from our lips should cause our brothers to stumble. I know times may get rough. Things may not go your way. No matter what the circumstances you go through, whether good or bad, God said He would never leave you. Always remember that. Pray for guidance through those circumstances.

ALL THE PREACHER'S WIVES
A Peek Behind The Curtain Of Being A Preacher's Wife

I am aware that not every pastor's wife will have the same type of life experiences as I have. Not all pastor's wives will have the kind of husband-leader that I have. I know, because my daughter had a totally different experience in being a pastor's wife as I do. I am blessed with a caring husband who shows respect and love for me. Now as with any situation, life is not always perfect. Even a bed of roses at one time had thorns. Like everyone else, we've had our disagreements, but thanks be to God, we worked them out. I know all pastors' wives can't say that. I am not trying to be boastful, just encouraging. Don't allow Satan to tear up your union based on one unimportant misunderstanding. Don't let anyone cause you to lose your faith in the Lord. Learn how to have Godly conversations with your spouse. No, I'm not talking about quoting scriptures back and forth. I mean to speak and listen with care and compassion. Be mindful of what the other person may be thinking or feeling. Be willing to step outside of your comfort zone to see things from their perspective. God's relationship with us is a replica of what our marriage should look like. He displays unconditional love for us, even when we don't deserve it. He doesn't turn us away with each mistake we make. We should have the same level of compassion as our spouses. Not only will it positively affect our time together, but it will build a stronger ministry. A braided cord of three is much stronger than a single cord of one.

As you are reading this, I pray you understand that this is not to indicate perfection. Being a pastor's wife is a role where mistakes will be made and misunderstandings will be had. But the importance lies in how we handle them. Other women do not want a perfect role model. Other women are looking for a real Christian role model to relate to if they are serious about being a woman of God. Perfection will never be attained on this side of the Earth. Women are looking for down-to-earth women with real problems. They want someone who has similar problems to what they have. They will watch how you handle things. When they see how you deal with difficulties, it reaffirms that they can make it through hard times too. Your behavior is part of their life experiences helping to mold them into who they are to become. So live, learn, and love the role you have been chosen for.

ALL THE PREACHER'S WIVES
A Peek Behind The Curtain Of Being A Preacher's Wife

If I had to leave a nugget of advice to someone coming after me, it would be the following: Be yourself, genuine and sincere without pretense. Others are not looking for an impossible role model to try to pattern their life after. Who wants to strive toward an unreachable goal? Who wants to strive to be fake? Realness will win out every time. Don't waste time comparing yourself with others. God molded you to be you. No one else can be better than you at that. Moreover, the only person you should be in competition with is yourself five minutes ago. Compare yourself to yourself to see the growth He has allowed you to experience. You may be utterly surprised. Be determined to look your best with what is available to you. You do not have to spend a million dollars to look like it. Your beauty comes from within. I said earlier, He made us in His image. That is what we should display to others. So, focus on the God reflection others see in you. It is far more beautiful than the most expensive apparel. And lastly, take care of those entrusted to you. This includes your spouse (the pastor) and yourself. Both are equally important and instrumental to the growth of His ministry. Don't do anything that would hinder you from carrying out your mission in the ministry. Be present but observe your presence. What I mean is that you should be present and participate in the ministry, but at the same time, watch your actions to ensure they line up with your mission. You can't be always everywhere, and you shouldn't desire to be. But instead, be exactly where He wants you to be. There is only one place on His display shelf for the vessel you are becoming. Present your attributes humbly, yet proudly.

ALL THE PREACHER'S WIVES
A Peek Behind The Curtain Of Being A Preacher's Wife

Apostle Chosen Boston

"As a Preacher's wife, what would otherwise be considered abnormal behavior somehow evolves into the new normal."

ALL THE PREACHER'S WIVES
A Peek Behind The Curtain Of Being A Preacher's Wife

14
LOST WHILE UNDER THE INFLUENCE

"Where am I?" "How did I get here?" "Who am I?" I'm trapped in a dark place where I am all alone, but I'm not alone because I hear a deep vibrating sound of an echo of rhythm thumbing in thin air. Attempting to probe into where it's coming from, I then began to discover it was the sound of a heartbeat. Imprecise on how I got here? As voices echoed from outside penetrating this deep darkness…"Osafo maame, Osafo maame Osafo maame." It became louder like a magnetic force pulling me into the consciousness of the outside world. [Osafo maame is interpreted as "Pastor's wife" in Ghana in the Twi Tribe language].

Looking into the eyes of a gentleman staring back at me, tapping on my shoulder he utters, "Osafo is calling for you." As I rose up with haste from the couch inside the Pastor's office, I began to look down at my body starting from my arms and examining my clothes down to my feet. Touching my face, I began pondering how and when did I arrive in this body.

Let me take you behind the curtains of my life.

ALL THE PREACHER'S WIVES
A Peek Behind The Curtain Of Being A Preacher's Wife

As he was urgently approaching, I thought to myself, "There he is. There goes my 5'8", dark chocolate, slim, jet-black bushy hair, smooth skin husband, the Pastor." As I admired my husband affectionately peering at him through eyes of love and insurmountable respect, I was compelled to honor him as a wife should through a perpetual flow of submission.

He spoke, "My wife, why don't you take the children and go home and prepare dinner. I'm going to stay back to pray for a couple of hours".

I proudly responded, "No problem my husband." I continued, "Where are the keys?"

I walked over to the desk and grabbed the keys. I turned around and, with an almost mystic-like movement, a kiss was gently planted on my forehead and then upon the back of my right hand. I smiled as a flood of peace overwhelmed my heart.

Speaking once again, he said, "My wife, drive safe. I love you."

Humbled, I responded with, "I love you too."

I then departed out of the door.

As I was arranging the children in the car, I suddenly saw a vision: A promiscuous woman dressed in the attire of a harlot coming to meet with the pastor, my husband. I was startled by what I had seen. Getting into the family vehicle, I began to pray silently in my mind as I drove home. "Father, guard the eyes of my husband diligently and set no worthless thing before him. Keep his heart, mind, and body surrounded by your presence, and keep him in line with Your will for his life. Keep the spirit of Jesus within the heart of your servant that he will love you with all of his heart, mind, and soul. Any agent of darkness disguised as an ill-intentioned woman, I hereby declare the instant termination of your assignment, scheme, plot, or plan in the mighty name of Jesus."

"Dinner is ready!" I resounded. As the children ran down the stairs racing to the dinner table, my husband arrived, walking through the front door of our home. I said excitedly, "Welcome home honey".

"Thank you, my wife," he replied. "What's for dinner?"

"Your favorite" I replied.

We sat at the dinner table, prayed, and began eating. Shortly after we sat, the phone rang. My husband excused himself from the table, leaving me and the children.

As a Preacher's wife, what would otherwise be considered abnormal behavior somehow evolves into the new normal. Quality time with your family often suffers. Information that was shared with my husband on the account of counseling can never be shared with members of the congregation. Being a preacher's wife is a ministry all in itself. It is a calling. The Pastor's wife is a prominent figure in his life, and she plays the greatest role in his success or failure. As a pastor's wife, you must be prepared to learn and adapt on-the-fly to assist your husband and the ministry.

ALL THE PREACHER'S WIVES
A Peek Behind The Curtain Of Being A Preacher's Wife

My husband was essentially on call 24/7. Vacations, dates, outings, and fun for our family were rare. My husband was constantly running to address the cries of members often in the middle of the night. Our personal time as a couple and as a family was interrupted regularly.

"Honey, come. I have prepared your bath." I anticipated a response but there was none. Instead, all I heard was laughter coming from the other room, as though he was on the phone.

I would often find myself alone in the bathtub crying and praying to God. "Why... why God? What have I done to deserve this manner of life?" I worked to create a peaceful atmosphere, but I wasn't at peace internally. I worked to develop a warm and loving home, but I was treated coldly. "Strengthen me, Lord. Help me to carry out my role. For your grace is sufficient for me in my weakness".

As I prepared for bed I looked over at the clock. It showed 11:52 pm. I walked down the stairs to say goodnight, but my husband gestured that he didn't want to be disturbed. I turned around and headed to bed. There were many cold nights I lay there tossing and turning in bed alone. I remember saying to myself, "I didn't get married just to sleep alone. I'd rather be single instead of married and alone."

I looked over at the clock. The time showed 4:25 am.

"Will he ever come to bed?" I would ask myself. On countless nights I had to hold myself to fall asleep. This hurts so bad. I would pray, "God deliver me from this emotional neglect." Tears would roll down my face as I laid there attempting to listen to his conversation.

ALL THE PREACHER'S WIVES
A Peek Behind The Curtain Of Being A Preacher's Wife

I overheard my husband giving counsel to a member regarding how she should treat her husband. Apparently, they were having marital issues. It sounded as if her husband was having an affair with other women at work. My husband was giving sound biblical teachings, offering prayer and prophetic instruction.

People outside of our house might assume that I was privy to any information that was shared with my husband in private, but his ears were not my ears. Whatever was shared with him in private remained confidential. Likewise, he did not tell me every single thing about every single member. He believed in protecting information given to him as the pastor. As his wife, I did not hear and know everything shared with him. It should not be surprising that I'm not familiar with member secrets.

Moreover, depending on his level of maturity he will know how to balance information correctly given to him, which shouldn't affect his own quality of life and family. There came several times when information was shared with my husband on the account of counseling. Unfortunately, our life had become the very thing that he often counseled couples to avoid. At times, these issues escalated into disputes and disagreements between the two of us.

As I struggled to go back to sleep. He later climbed into bed around 6 am.

When married to a pastor, expect a bunch of late nights, early mornings, and loss of sleep. It will take a woman who understands the calling and assignment of her husband to be in such a position. Unfortunately, I preferred a normal life just like everyone else. I longed to get 8 hours of proper sleep every night.

ALL THE PREACHER'S WIVES
A Peek Behind The Curtain Of Being A Preacher's Wife

That morning I walked into the kitchen as usual. The boys had beaten me downstairs. I asked, "Good morning boys are you ready for breakfast?" Their response was expected, "Yes, mommy." Immediately after finishing breakfast as our customs were in our home, we had morning devotion.

"Come, let us have our family devotion, daddy should be coming down any minute," I spoke.

Every day was unpredictable. I never knew what to expect and what mood my husband would be in due to having so many responsibilities associated with the church and the members. Repeatedly, it left me confused and unsettled.

When he came downstairs, I asked, "Baby how do I look," while walking, twisting, and strutting in front of the mirrors in hope of his approval of my appearance.

He replied, "You know I don't like those Jezebel items."

I was stunned. I swallowed loudly and looked at him with discomfort. I countered, "Excuse me? So, what exactly are you saying?"

"All women who wear such things are going to hell because they are daughters of Jezebel, the mother of harlots. The same goes for all the women who are preaching in the pulpit calling themselves apostles, pastors, prophets, teachers, evangelists, etc. The lake of fire is waiting for such," he disclosed.

"My husband, how could you say that?" I argued. "Show me In the Bible where it's written if you wear jewelry, make-up, trousers, weaves, etc., you are going to hell or the product of Jezebel."

He grabbed the Bible and began to expound. We stayed in our house for hours searching the scriptures, going back and forth, and reasoning through the scriptures. "He's a master at his craft no wonder he's a pastor who can convince his sheep to follow his lead even against their own will," I discreetly thought to myself.

We both looked at the clock and realized it was now time to pick the children up from school. After hours of arguing the scriptures, I agreed, grudgingly, to what he was teaching. Weeks later I noticed my wardrobe started to change. My appetite for jewelry, make-up and trousers left me because I wanted to please my husband and to be attractive to him. I thirsted to live in peace. In the process, I was being brainwashed and reprogrammed into an image I could not identify.

I arrived at the school and found the children. They saw the car and said, "Hey, mommy!"

I asked, "Hey baby, how was school?"

"School was good." My son replied. "Today we discussed our parents and the work they do," the youngest son said.

"Awesome son I bet you were excited to speak about the work your parents do". I spoke.

"Mommy I wasn't happy because I couldn't tell the class what my daddy did for a living," he responded. As I looked over at my husband with a look of discouragement. I knew something must change.

"Are you hungry?" I asked.

"Yes, mommy". My son replied.

"Today I will cook," my husband said.

"Yay!" Screamed the children.

"Daddy, we want fufu and light soup," the boys requested.

"What do you want to eat tonight mommy?" My husband asked me.

"Yes, I'll take fufu and light soup," I responded as his phone rang.

A member of the ministry was calling. I could hear crying on the other side of the phone. My husband excused himself. Even though his ears were not my ears, his pain became my pain. The question was how would I respond to the pain I knew he was experiencing? This became an opportunity for me to honor God. To steward pain well, it helps to shape our posture in painful times of ministry,

One of the most critical decisions you can make in ministry is how you steward pain. Seasons of pain can generate cycles of destructive personal patterns, but pain can also be a furnace of refinement. Take a look at Prov. 17:3; 1 Pet. 4:12–19.

ALL THE PREACHER'S WIVES
A Peek Behind The Curtain Of Being A Preacher's Wife

I have not known a more painful period in my 12 years in ministry than the 6th year in ministry, which led up to our divorce. I've witnessed my husband, a lead pastor, honorably carry out his responsibilities and prayerfully consider decisions in a tumultuous year of no-win scenarios. Yet, he was always grateful to see the provision of the Lord which often surprised us.

Coming home from the grocery store, I heard the shower running in our master bedroom. I yelled, "Honey, I'm home," but there was no response. I entered the kitchen and discovered his phone lying on the kitchen countertop open. It was playing the auto-Bible app of the King James Version, 1 Corinthians 10.

I sat the groceries bags down to prepare to cook. I began excitedly listening to the Bible. I decided to replay it and keep it on repeat. So, I grabbed the phone of my husband. I reached out to press repeat and immediately a text message came across the screen. "I love you so much I want to marry someone like you." This was the text message. Another text comes through with a sexually suggestive picture from the same number. I dropped the phone back onto the counter and grabbed it at my heart. I thought to myself, "What could this mean?" It felt as if an elephant was suddenly sitting on my chest, listening to my racing heartbeat. I sat to gather myself. Many thoughts started running through my head. Suddenly, I heard his footsteps coming down the stairs. "My wife, have seen my phone?" He yelled. "Over there in the kitchen dear". I replied.

He walked over to where I was seated and grabbed me from behind and kissed me on my neck. Then, he took my hand into his own, walked me up the stairs into our master bedroom, and we made love.

"Your body is not your own it belongs to your husband and your husband's body is not his own, it body belongs to you." (1 Corinthians:7). This is what the Bible tells us regarding marriage but serving your husband intimately and sexually is not always easy, especially when you are habitually neglected, lonely, and despised. There are seasons when you may feel like a sex dummy. It's when he uses you for sex and instantly returns to acting as if you never existed. It's when you wish those moments of pleasure were extended to every other time within the marriage, but it isn't.

When we are under attack or feeling like we are drowning in a stormy sea, sometimes all we can do is cry out to God praying for rescue. The same God who rescues you from sin and death can rescue you from a stormy season of ministry. That may not mean that your circumstances change or that the storm stops immediately. Rescue may mean that He calms your raging emotions, protects you from bitterness, or offers you perseverance so that you can continue to serve.

"Baby I am called into ministry just like you," I spoke. "Before we got married, I was single and working in ministry. I had been called and chosen. God separated me as the Bible describes separating the wheat from the chaff. He consecrated me and molded me into His faithful servant.". I resounded. "I've been a faithful, supportive, loving, helpful, and patient wife to you, our children, and the ministry. The master has need of me." I shouted.

The words continued to flow as the tears trailed the outlines of my face. I declared, "You deceived me. You told me a woman cannot preach in the house of God. All these many years I was married to you faithfully, but you wanted to shut me up. You wanted to muzzle the ox that treads the corn. Quite frankly, when you are chosen by God, there's no devil in hell that can stop the hand of God upon your life." I looked at him one final time and left for my favorite place in the home. I entered my closet, shut the door, and prayed.

As the sun began to set, I returned to our bed and found myself falling suddenly into a deep and sudden sleep. Suddenly in an unexpected dream, I saw a majestic woman standing before me. Her garments were flowing as if to a breeze that I could not feel and resplendent. The woman had power and authority. And then she looked at me…

She said, "Daughter of Zion if you do not do the will of God, you will be damned." I was instantly filled with fear and woke up. But afterward, the interpretation of the dream washed over me. I knew she was sent to give me a warning against abandoning the purpose and will of God for my life. I turned to my husband and said, "Honey…honey wake up! I just had a dream."

"Tell me the dream my wife" he murmured. He listened nonchalantly and immediately went back to sleep. Suddenly, I couldn't sleep. I stayed up and prayed for counsel and wisdom from God concerning the dream. Quite frankly, there were often moments when my husband appeared to show more care and concern about the sheep - his congregation, and their spiritual development, purpose, overall well-being, and balance of life than he cared for same regarding his own wife and children. The Church had become the pastor's wife.

The health and success of the church and the health and success of our families are linked. Family life is significantly important to the well-being of the church. If families are not healthy and vibrant, the church will not be healthy and vibrant. It is imperative for pastors and leaders to set an example in this regard. There are, however, no qualifications for the pastor's wife and children listed. Yet, our churches are full of people with unreasonable and demanding expectations of the pastor's family. The wife is expected to serve in certain leadership and service roles in a church. The children are commonly expected to perform for the congregation with a maturity they may not yet possess and the ability to interact with adults in a way that is much more advanced than most other children. Rarely have I met a pastor's wife and children who do not feel this immense pressure. Many eventually grow to resent it or, better still, feel like it's a curse.

"How did I get trapped here? You promised me that we would do ministry together. You said I would work ministry along said you. In the beginning, before we got married, you encouraged the giftings of God inside me. You told me I was a great Prophetess of God and I have a bright future. I am not just a shadow of my husband," I stated. "Why have I become your doormat? God did not call me to leave me here in this God-forsaken marriage." I walked away into my prayer closet, fell to my knees, and prayed, "God please deliver me from this marriage."

I remember the time I cried out to God and said, "Father, I don't know how you are going to do it, but I need you to deliver me. I am dying inside. There's no one to talk to and nowhere to run. I am stuck Lord, and I need your help." I would run to my closet to pray at all hours of the day. Sometimes right after church I would isolate myself and cry and pray. At that point in my life, I became completely sold out to my husband and wholeheartedly abandoned the calling of God upon my life. I stopped doing my own ministry all to push, support, and build his ministry. Many times, when I tried to rise up to do what I was mandated to do, my husband would raise up against it like a lion ready to devour its prey. I was caged, I was held back, stopped, and blocked from doing what God called and chose me to do.

There were horrifying nights and days of quarrels, and then the abuse set in. From emotional abuse to spiritual abuse, from spiritual abuse to mental abuse, and lastly physical abuse. This was the final straw.

You looked ahead to Sunday and all your energy was immediately drained. You tried to think through the list of things that needed to get done before the pre-church morning rush, but your mind was suddenly too distracted. Your family received one blow after another. This had become my life. I couldn't reach out to the church for help. I also did not want to tarnish my husband's image with the congregations of our churches. So, I reluctantly reached out to a trusted pastor-friend to discuss the new behavior and mood in our home. It was a great shock to him. I scheduled a time to meet with them face-to-face, but this didn't save us. Unfortunately, the abuse escalated and spread not only to me but also to the physical abuse of our children. Calls were made to the police several times. Child protective services were called on my husband. He was eventually arrested. This was a tremendous blow to our family, but we were also in desperate need of help.

"I felt so trapped". There had even been times when I'd thought about killing myself. There was a time I also escaped out of the window with our small children to find safety while he was sleeping just to return home. I was tired of the hypocrisy, and pretentious living. I had lost my true identity, I was physically numb, and I had been abused spiritually to such an extreme degree that I was left dumbfounded. Today, I recognize that not everyone survives these circumstances. Eventually, I found the courage to file for divorce.

As I stated before, being a pastor's wife is a calling; you must be ready and prepared for it. My children and I found safety though the marriage ended with a divorce. Today, both of us are on the journey of healing and wholeness. We decided that co-parenting was the best option.

"I love the LORD, because he has heard my voice and my pleas for mercy. Because he inclined his ear to me, therefore I will call on him as long as I live. The snares of death encompassed me; the pangs of Sheol laid hold on me; I suffered distress and anguish. Then I called on the name of the LORD: 'O LORD, I pray, deliver my soul!' Gracious is the LORD, and righteous; our God is merciful.

"The LORD preserves the simple; when I was brought low, he saved me. Return, O my soul, to your rest; for the LORD has dealt bountifully with you." (Psalms 166:1-7)

ALL THE PREACHER'S WIVES
A Peek Behind The Curtain Of Being A Preacher's Wife

My name is Prophetess Chosen Boston, and this is the story of my life as a Preacher's wife.

ALL THE PREACHER'S WIVES
A Peek Behind The Curtain Of Being A Preacher's Wife

Josie Cooper

"I grew up in the projects and I encountered some of the same types of environments that many experienced such as drugs, alcohol, watching my neighbors fight, parties, etc. The best thing my mother did for me was to expose me to her individual way of living."

ALL THE PREACHER'S WIVES
A Peek Behind The Curtain Of Being A Preacher's Wife

15
PRODUCTS OF OUR ENVIRONMENT

As I began writing this story about my journey in being married to a pastor, the process brought back many memories I will be sharing with you. While writing, I've experienced an entire spectrum of emotions: feelings of joy, happiness, gladness, sadness, and even peace. Proverbs 17:22 tells us "A merry heart does good like medicine, but a broken spirit dries the bones." There are elements of my story that may cause you to laugh but, most of all, I pray you will be strengthened, encouraged, and inspired.

I never sought to become a pastor's wife. My life took many twists and turns for me to have finally arrived where I am today mentally, spiritually, and emotionally. One of the greatest gifts I gained through my life experience is the ability to find serenity regardless of the circumstance. So, for now, I encourage you to sit back and enjoy as I tell my story about being a pastor's wife.

I remember as a child at the age of seven I had a dream that I was preaching, and the subject was 'You can't hide from God". I used the illustrations about Adam and Eve hiding in the garden and about Jonah running away and being caught in the belly of the fish. I immediately went into the kitchen and shared my dream with my mother. Typically, a seven-year-old child knows little about

ALL THE PREACHER'S WIVES
A Peek Behind The Curtain Of Being A Preacher's Wife

constructing a sermon. This alone shocked my mother yet being a minister herself, she knew exactly what God was calling me to do. I was raised in the church, yet I still wasn't sure what it all meant. By the time I was a teenager I knew I was called to preach but I would spend a few years running, not from God but from the assignment and call on my life.

I grew up with my mom and my dad who loved me dearly. I am the youngest of six children - Sallie, Phillis, Edna, Richard Earl (who passed away at 5 months), Shelton (RIP) who had my heart, and me. We didn't have much yet we had love and each other.

I grew up in the projects and I encountered some of the same types of environments that many experienced such as drugs, alcohol, watching my neighbors fight, parties, etc. The best thing my mother did for me was to expose me to her individual way of living. My mother was a living example of what it was to be a wife, mother, and a Christian woman of God. If my mother would not have been the woman she was and taught us the right way to live life, I am certain I would have been a victim of my surroundings. Many days I could not wait for the opportunity to lie down to daydream and visualize a better life for myself. Oh, how I wanted to get away and succeed so desperately. I wanted to be grown and live on my own. As a child, some affectionally called me Ms. Josie because I carried a little purse, and I was already being told I was mature for my age.

I met my husband when I was the president of our young adult choir that we both were a part of. He was friendly, funny, laughed often, and had a smile with dimples. I could tell he had a crush on me and, although he was four years older, it was mutual. Because his birthday was approaching, I threw him a party at Pizza Hut and all the young people were there from our church. After that night, we began talking regularly on the phone. I remember one night we had talked all night long and I heard my daddy get up for work and come down the hallway. I tried to tell him I had to go because my dad was coming but he kept on talking. I said it a little louder, "I have to go. My daddy is coming!" I quickly threw my head down on the side of the couch and let the phone fall on the floor. The next thing I heard was my dad in his deep voice saying to me, "Josie you better not still be on that phone!" With my eyes half open, I began yawning as if I was just waking up. I knew my dad would whoop my behind if he knew I had been on the phone all night. He put the fear of God in us, yet I loved him for it. Soon after that, we began dating. We both were really into learning more about God. We did not miss Bible study on Wednesdays or church on Sundays. Our Pastor encouraged us and eventually married us. I was seventeen and he was twenty-one. My parents signed their consent. Yes, I was only seventeen. lol.

When my husband told me he was called to preach I was nervous. He loves to talk, and I was so afraid that he was going to get up there and say the wrong thing. I didn't want to preach, and I wasn't sure if I wanted him to either. We got along so well and were doing good; I didn't want to mess things up. I also began to realize that with spiritual elevation and promotion we would also encounter greater spiritual attacks. Who really wants that part of growth? Not me!

Married preachers?

I eventually surrendered to my calling, though reluctantly. I didn't look like a typical female preacher. Most church women looked plain simple with no makeup or plain overweight and wore long dresses. Oh no! I would not fit in! Surely, I would be seen as a Jezebel with my jewelry, makeup, and pants. I was willing to conform and bend a little, yet I had to be true to myself. God made us uniquely to walk in our individuality. My older sister told me she said, "Josie God knew who you were before he called you. You will fine. Just be yourself." (Thanks Sallie! I still remember that).

As life would have it the day of the sermon, we got into an argument. I went to see a childhood girlfriend to get my mind off of it. At the service, he gave accolades to his beautiful young wife as if we

ALL THE PREACHER'S WIVES
A Peek Behind The Curtain Of Being A Preacher's Wife

had not been arguing earlier. I don't even remember what the argument was about. Honestly, it was probably a result of the stress and tension of the event. It is important to stay on one accord because the devil will try to divide a husband and wife, especially when God is about to bless you both. When he attended a theology school, I studied along with him. We didn't want to be preachers that couldn't preach. Lol

He pastored several churches before we started a church. We brought the land and built it from the ground up. We made a lot of sacrifices for the ministry. During those early years, he could not decide whether I needed to wear skirts, dresses, suits, or short pants. I found it difficult to keep track of public opinion. After all, I was only in my twenties, and I wasn't trying to look like an old lady in my pictures. Ironically, people tell me now that it appears that I'm aging backward. I say "No," I just started out looking older, anointed, and well-seasoned. Lol

After preaching for a little while we were both still on fire for God and willing to do whatever it was that he called us to do. However, we were not prepared for the trials, temptations, wiles of the devil, and spiritual wickedness in high places that would eventually divide us. People are always watching, judging, criticizing, and complaining. Women, in particular, will scrutinize you the most. They will judge your fashion, style, hair, makeup, and physical appearance.

In order to be a pastor's wife, one must be prepared spiritually, mentally, and emotionally. If you are interested in just being glamorous then go into modeling. A pastor's wife must be a prayer warrior and secure in who you are. Equally important is to remember that you are more than your body and attractive looks. " Charm is deceitful and beauty is passing, but a woman that fears the Lord, she shall be praised" Proverbs 31:30 (NKJV). Many feel that all you need to do is be classy, dress fashionably well, smile frequently, and look beautiful. Oh, and please don't exert your opinion much. You are expected to get along with everyone and if there's something that you don't like, you must be quiet and take it to the Lord in prayer. For this reason, it is crucial that you choose your confidants wisely. Unfortunately, many husbands will not be receptive to hearing you complain or expressing your concerns about things that you may perceive may be an asset to him.

We collectively decided to always be supportive and not criticize. You both are on the same team. Sometimes it may not feel like it. Speak the truth in love when it comes to our efforts for the kingdom. Because we both preached, we did not allow people to compare our preaching styles whether it involved articulation, the ability to rightly divide the word, or your charismatic ability to stir a crowd. All these things could be placed up for debate. If you are not careful, you will be in competition with the very one whom you are supposed to be in partnership with. Complement each other by choosing not to compete.

These are a few things to keep in mind: *

1. Maintain your personal relationship with God through prayer, fasting, and reading God's Word.
2. His calling is his and you are there as his biggest support mechanism.
3. Represent GOD in him and in all that you are as best as you can. (You are his eye candy)
4. When he is stressed, share only what is necessary and use discretion. This is called wisdom.
5. Love Him but most importantly, respect him.
6. Never embarrass him in public. You can deal with issues privately.
7. Members are sheep and they go astray. Be his listening ear and don't fuel the fire.
8. Learn how to hold your peace and when to speak. Regarding other women, see what you see, know what you know, and hold fast to your position firmly.

ALL THE PREACHER'S WIVES
A Peek Behind The Curtain Of Being A Preacher's Wife

9. Keep him interested in the bedroom and do not share how good he is, or any lack thereof, with anyone unless it is a professional. Be a lady in public yet creative in the bedroom. He is YOUR husband, so minister to him in a way only you can.
10. Know your worth and Do Not tolerate Physical or emotional abuse. It is not OK! I pray none of you ever have to deal with it. He has been called to love you as Christ loves the church. Do not settle for less. There is no prestige, no amount of money, no large enough house, jewelry, or designer bags, or clothing to withstand being emotionally or physically abused. Period.

My husband and I divorced after 25 years of marriage. God has been gracious to us and given us each the fortitude to each move in a healthier direction.

Meanwhile, God presented me with a second time around and I'm very grateful for my love! I am married to my wonderful husband Elder James Cooper. God has blessed us with a blended family of four sons. We serve in ministry together. God is truly amazing!

Our ministry consists of JJJ Love Ministries where we touch lives all over the world! We are able to feed the hungry through JC Cook's with Love Food truck. Our beauty salon Kutn Up Salon and Body Sculpting is also a part of our ministry, helping people to look and feel better about themselves. I am a recording artist, and now thanks to *All The Preacher's Wives*, I am now a published author too! I needed the motivation to move higher.

Enjoy life, and live and be happy. Being a pastor's wife is a Blessing! Take every smile you can get. " The thief comes to kill steal and destroy but I come that you may have life more abundantly." John 10:10 (KJV). Learn to appreciate all the good times without harboring resentment, grudges, and bitterness. These things will stifle the joy that God has promised you. For we all have sinned and come short of the glory of God. You married a human with flaws like yourself. We all need God to strengthen and encourage us. I pray that you both will maximize your abilities, individually and collectively. Two can be a powerful force in the world if you stay in one accord. The devil will try you both, but it is up to you all to let him win.

Be thankful if you are chosen for this calling. Many may not make it, but prayerfully you will. May God bless you. I wish you success and blessings in your endeavors, and may you be the greatest wife and woman of God that he has created you to be.

"Beloved I wish above all things that you mayest prosper and be in health even as your soul prosperity." 3John 1:2(KJV)

Love, forgive, fast, and Pray. Repeat Repeat Repeat

In HIS Service
Pastor Josie Braxton Cooper

ALL THE PREACHER'S WIVES
A Peek Behind The Curtain Of Being A Preacher's Wife

Petra

"You are miserable covering for him. You say nothing to no one because you cannot talk to anyone, especially people in the church. In your heart you want to protect him… in your head, you want to leave him."

ALL THE PREACHER'S WIVES
A Peek Behind The Curtain Of Being A Preacher's Wife

16
FOR THE LOVE OF GOD

What do you do when you are disrespected? What do you do when you are overlooked? I bet you didn't expect those questions, especially coming from a pastor's wife. Why not? These are real issues that we sometimes have to contend with. So, what do you do? You hold your head up high and smile...because you are the pastor's wife.

He did not receive his calling until after we were married. Our lives had already begun, and I did not see this as a part of it. He never indicated that he would be a minister or servant of the Lord. As unexpected as it was, I was concerned that his calling was sincere. I prayed the Lord called him and not his aunt. I know that sounds bad, but it seemed as though she may have been grooming him to be a preacher. All I knew to do was pray. But I was not prepared for what his calling would mean to me.

At times, he would tell me what his next sermon would be. I don't know if this was common among other pastors and their spouses, but I felt uncomfortable in "critiquing" his sermon. I would just say let that be between you and the Lord. ("Except the Lord build the house, they labor in vain." Psalm 127:1 King James Study Bible) I wanted to experience the Word of the Lord at the same time the parishioners did. Was this going to be my calling? I had not received this from Him, and this made me feel awkward about hearing his sermon first.

ALL THE PREACHER'S WIVES
A Peek Behind The Curtain Of Being A Preacher's Wife

Some people misunderstand the life of the ministry. The assumptions that people have are unrealistic. "They have a good marriage," "what a loving couple they are," "they look so good together because he is a pastor." These are some of the things they said about our relationship. "He is a dynamic messenger." "He looks good in the pulpit," "His robe hangs just right, and he prays so well." All of that just may be true. Some of it may be a façade. They couldn't see what the relationship was really like. They could not see what the robe was hiding. If they only knew the truth.

The truth is often unimaginable. You are miserable covering for him. You say nothing to no one because you cannot talk to anyone, especially people in the church. In your heart you want to protect him… in your head, you want to leave him. An internal conflict you deal with daily. You do not want to blemish his reputation. What goes on at home should stay at home. But what if you need help at home? To whom do you turn? Home can be hell. He is a gossip, liar, poor money manager, and a pretender. He does not analyze the facts and possesses no sense of discernment. These aspects are why I doubted the origin of his "calling." His birth family runs him. But unlike him, they cannot run me, and that just might be the problem.

The church is a show for his family. Who can sing, pray, and bring the Word the best? This is what the mission of the services became. I could not proudly represent this. Worship service should be done with love for God and not praise for man. Sure, they do a good job, but it is for the wrong reasons. They want something in return, they want control. Control over everything and everybody. I do not get paid for my efforts or my duties. Nor do I desire to. God gives me the opportunity to work outside the home, I am still employed and for that, I am thankful.

It was my time to teach Sunday school, and things were going well. In walks his aunt bringing guests. She crosses my path with the guests and said, "do not mind her, she is not doing anything." I could not believe the level of disrespect she displayed before her guests. She comes back and talks loudly to her guests. One of the guests encourages her to lower her voice. Yes, the guest wanted to be respectful. But this did not dissuade her from interrupting. We are about to close out Sunday school and I ask for any closing comments. Ole Auntie jumps up and rambles on and on. I politely say "Sister, time is far spent." She tells me "you have had your say now I will have mine." I am stunned. When she finishes, I close Sunday school with a prayer of forgiveness for me. I gather my things and leave. I call my best friend and tell her I just do not want to fight an old lady. I am so upset I start to cry. That has never happened to me before. I am so angry that I'm to the point of tears. There is no going back from this. The thin fragile relationship we had exists no more. My friend insists I come to her home. I get there and she opens the door and says, "Come in little buckeroo, come to Big sis." I am a mess. I begin, "I hate that bitch! I am done." I meant it too. There is no coming back from this one. She and my husband can kiss anything that remotely looked like a relationship goodbye. Oh, it is no great loss. No more gifts or money, no more acknowledgments, no none. She has cut my olive branch off for the last time.

"If possible, so far as it depends on you, live peaceably with all." (Romans 12:18, ESV)

After several days of avoiding me, my husband does not want to address the issues. He tells me that this is between me and his aunt. I express that I am relieved. Now I know where I stand with you. I can handle myself especially when I know who my enemies are. Well, let us remember, he is the Pastor, and I am the wife. "Husbands, love your wives, even as Christ also loved the church, and gave himself for it. (Ephesians 5:25 King James Study Bible)

It is not enough to care for the home, work, and children, which includes assisting with homework and attending mid-week service. He must also love and care for his wife, protecting her from all perceivable hurt and harm. One of the things I found difficult to accept is his lack of planning and preparation. He drives like a bat out of hell to get us all to mid-week service. I do not enjoy and never have enjoyed riding with people who speed. What is the rush, Pastor? "I just do not want to be late," he states. I responded with, "You do this every week, and you know I am not comfortable with you speeding. Just leave before time. This is simple math." But no matter how early or late we arrive, we start late because he was waiting on his consistently late aunt to arrive. This makes my blood boil. I gently nudged, "if you start on time they will arrive on time." "Let me get things in order" is always his excuse.

But submission and sacrifice to the pastor is not all we are expected to do. When we get back home from mid-week service, baths must be done. The night routine must be completed, and usually it is left up to me to make sure it is done. In the meantime, someone forgot to tell me about a project that needs to be done for tomorrow. Most parents know what this means because we have all probably run into this at least once in the lives of our children. But compounded with the struggle of keeping my marriage intact and the ministry flourishing when they are being overrun by family, the run-of-the-mill motherly duties become overwhelming.

As the pastor's wife I work to have peace within my life. To keep down confusion, I started driving the kids and me to church at a safe speed – slowly. Auntie continued to be slow. I gently nudge by suggesting "The people who make it on time deserve to be treated as if their time matters. If you start on time the late ones will start getting there on time." Yes, I was being redundant and possibly slightly a nuisance in his opinion, but it was an answer to a prayer. I asked God how I can support and encourage my husband without appearing negative, and these words are what He gave me. I was apprehensive at first, then I remembered the source. Therefore, this Word from God deserved to be repeated. "Get wisdom, get understanding; forget it not; neither decline from the words of my mouth." (Proverbs 4:5 King James Study Bible)

ALL THE PREACHER'S WIVES
A Peek Behind The Curtain Of Being A Preacher's Wife

With the lateness of the hour approaching and all the kids' chores suddenly becoming my responsibility, I eventually decided to stop attending mid-week services. I explained my position to my husband, "The children are getting in bed later, and homework is not being completed until late. It is not fair to them or me." He did not agree, but I could not possibly get both done. So I would have to offer my support in ways other than my presence.

My concerns were confirmed when I happened to speak with a gentleman. I believe a friend of mine knew him or knew of him, and she said, "I saw your wife last Wednesday leaving the church." He insisted, "She could not have seen her because my wife does not attend mid-week service. It is too hard on her and the kids. It is rare for her to attend weekday-anything at church because of the kids." I smiled but did not share my story for I truly understood his wife's position. My friend kept searching her mind convinced she had seen her. He adamantly expressed that his wife had not been at the church. This further influenced me to stay home and take care of the duties. So being the wife of a preacher does not mean you can or should be at all services or events. You must care for your house before you can care for God's house.

Keeping a clean house did not end with our home. Everyone does not have a large church with the benefits of having a cleaning crew or volunteers to clean consistently. There are certain areas that require more attention than others. I was the self-appointed cleaner. I didn't mind. I like a clean house so why wouldn't I want a clean church? My focus was the bathrooms and kitchen. I vacuumed periodically but told others they needed to assist with that. I had the kids to help and had help from my relatives. Auntie and her crew did nothing but walk around and point things out for me to do. I would get Pastor and tell him they needed his assistance. I expected him to protect me from the treatment of his aunt. Auntie wanted to deliver the word and be seen, but cleaning was not her thing. Instead, she continued to point out to me what needs to be done. No sir, that is not going to happen. I tried to let my husband handle the discord. But I was again disappointed.

ALL THE PREACHER'S WIVES
A Peek Behind The Curtain Of Being A Preacher's Wife

Then there were the physical aspects of being in the ministry. Everyone attempts to hug you, neighbor! I am not a fan of that greeting. A high five or a handshake is good for me. The side hug can be an option, but the full-on chest-to-chest, cheek-to-cheek hug was unnecessary. On one occasion the pastor instructed us to hug our neighbor, and this gentleman said to me, "Oh I know you are going to hug me," he grabbed me before I could side-hug him and yes, I felt uncomfortable. He was inappropriate with his touch. He smiled, I did not. After we arrived home, I told the pastor to rethink that gesture because everyone who comes to church is not looking for the Lord and some have little respect for the church. I told him about the situation, and he stated there is always someone who will ruin something innocent. That is what he thought I was doing? He simply did not get it. So, after that, I simply made my own greeting to protect myself. This was prior to Covid-19.

Covid-19 brought some good and bad things into everyone's lives. Items had to be sanitized, six feet distancing, mask worn and the sheltering in place and limiting the number of persons that could be in a building/or church. Some bad things that accompanied Covid-19 were the number of deaths and the isolation and loneliness of people. We are meant to commune. The slow and cautious lifting of restrictions taught us how much we valued others. However, the selfishness of others bothered me. The anti-maskers and anti-vaccinators. The mask protected us from one another. You from me and me from you. You cannot tell a person's health history just by looking at them. I know the pastors missed their congregations and the fellowship, they got inventive and started using technology they never dreamed they would be using. Some Pastors were fined for not complying with the mandate. They had too many members in their congregation present at that time. Pastors are leaders, in that leading you are to protect your flock and be good stewards of the money that is sown into the church. Paying a fine was wasting money. This pastor had an excuse for that one, he simply missed his congregation. I was surprised by him as well as others. Are we not to obey the laws of the land?

ALL THE PREACHER'S WIVES
A Peek Behind The Curtain Of Being A Preacher's Wife

This Pastor is not a great money manager. He has no respect for the needs of his household. He takes care of Auntie's debt and expects me to fill in the gap. In essence, I was working to take care of his aunt. No, that ship has sailed. After the disrespectful stance she took at church, my money stopped being the lifesaver. I constantly said in the past she is not a responsible money manager, and I am not, or should I say my money is not going to be saving her anymore. They thought I would cool off and change my mind. I stopped putting money into the joint saving account and put just enough into the checking account to assist with covering the household expenses. Good thing I kept my own accounts when we got married. As my grandmother says, keep something for yourself. I had a career when I met him. So, I was not depending on anyone, let alone a man. Looking back, he may have been looking at my career and had delusions I was doing well financially. I was doing what I wanted to do but I do not discuss my finances with others. My dad taught me that. No one needs to know what is in your pocket. I had great credit when I met him and a steady job, my own place, and a car. I guess I was a good catch. When the finance talk came up, I laid it on the line, I do not co-sign for people because I have been burned before. He asked if I would do that for him. I repeated my statement and added I do not know you like that. So, after we got married, I find out you feel indebted to take care of Auntie. That is why you need to discuss financial obligations prior to the union, even without disclosing what you do for yourself. With this revelation about his indebtedness, My response was, "that is your debt, not mine and if I had known this, the marriage never would have happened."

Dinner and fellowship go hand in hand with churches. It can be a great time when you have help. When I say help, I mean working help. My cousin volunteered once with the culinary committee. She turned out to me slyly lazy. She really does not want to work, but her husband is a deacon, so she felt obligated to step up. She decided to play with a baby to get out of actually working. The hostess asked her very nicely to give the baby up and to please come help. I giggled and grinned to myself. She got busted. She did not want to, but found herself ungraciously helping the committee.

One of my long-time friends volunteered to prepare dinner at the church, she was so proud of herself, she had her menu together and wanted to donate her time and resources to this meal. She did have volunteers and did ask others to chip in a dessert or two. I went back to check on her when the big day arrived, she was like Martha Stewart in that kitchen because she enjoys cooking. Well, we know Auntie cannot stay away. She went to the bathroom and found her way back to the kitchen. I was on table decorating duty. Jackie was in her element. She looked at the table of food, which was set up buffet style, then she saw a plate of egg halves. She asked me about them. "Baby girl, I have no idea where they came from." She goes ballistic, why are there seven egg halves? I was sorry, but I had to laugh, how do you get seven egg halves? She started cursing (in the church). I kept laughing, I tried hard to stop. She then says that Auntie should have kept that where she found it. She then picks them up and tosses them in the trash. "I have worked hard on this meal, and she is not going to have anyone leaving out of here saying they got food poisoning from here. And we both know she ate that half of the missing egg." Dinner went well, clean up went well, everyone was happy, and Jackie was very pleased. I thanked her profusely, for we know some jobs are thankless. You must show appreciation to others no matter how small or large the effort or work was placed into the job. Anything that a person has given or sown into you requires a thank you.

A Pastor's wife is always under the microscope. You must be always on your game. What you say, how you dress, what you participate in, how you present yourself is under a microscope. I come from a traditional Baptist church where you dressed up for church. So, I love hats and heels the whole nine. Auntie always looks me up and down and she makes it noticeable. My husband comes home and tells me my hat was too big, I counter with it, "my hat is pretty, and they cannot have it. How dare you come in here with that mess. They walk all over you, do not come back to me with anything they have to say.

ALL THE PREACHER'S WIVES
A Peek Behind The Curtain Of Being A Preacher's Wife

Because you and I both know they are going to be asking for money next week. My money is still off-limits to them. She disrespected me and you had nothing to say. I was done then, and I am still done now. Don't bring anything else to me from her. Especially her opinion regarding anything I wear or do. I am done." Pastor wants me to forgive and forget. I have sir. I have. Now you have an opinion, but it's too little too late.

Do not get me wrong, he preaches well. The Spirit of the Lord really comes in during the service. That I can feel and see. The power of the Lord cannot be beaten. I do not play about the church. I have worshipped despite the shenanigans. I also never thought I would be in a church where the family of the Pastor is the ones keeping up the discord. No, they all do not do it, there are others who are supportive of God's work, but the family should demonstrate love and support. I want him to take the lead and use correction when their actions go against the Word. They love confusion. Many of them have witnessed Auntie's attacks, yet neither do they offer any correction.

Rumor has it Pastor is flirting with someone; truth be told I do not care. I believe it but have never confronted him. The games people play. He had this woman bring this elaborate meal to the church for an anniversary dinner. This occurred twice. The second year she left and looked defeated. I know that look when a person makes you promises, and they never come to fruition. Why would you lead someone on like that? She left two items of expensive cookware and never came back to retrieve them. I asked a couple of times about the cookware; he never said a word. That confirmed it for me. A neighbor told me he was running around on his wife and was at a party. When he came out someone had thrown a brick through his windshield. He said he called the wrecker and had it towed home the following day. When the wrecker arrived his wife was looking out the window and she never asked about the car, that is when he knew she was the one who damaged his vehicle. He also told me she never did anything wrong in their marriage, it was all him. He said he was just being doggish. This demonstrated to me that a woman can be all a man needs, and he still can run around on her. He left me shaking my head. All I could say was to thine own self be true.

    The thread is bare on this relationship. Now do not act surprised. How much more am I to take and smile about it? I am not sure that counseling can help my situation. I do not wish to waste my time if he is not going to honestly try. What is the phrase? Heavy is the head that wears the crown. A façade of a marriage? But who kept chipping away at it? He has threatened to leave, and I simply say ok. Why am I still here? That I cannot truly answer. The kids need the two of us. They are delicate and often say they are glad they have both of their parents. The disrespectful lies and not having the backbone to stand up to his aunt is laughable. The women in the church and his family pump him up because their husbands could not tolerate them anymore.

I know there will be many who say you do not stay for the children or his position. But I have my own thoughts. I am comfortable in my skin. I know God will not put more on me than I can bare. God's perfect timing. "…. greater is He that is in me than he that is in the world." (1 John 4:4 King James Study Bible).

    So, I say to those reading my words. Just like any other woman, preachers' wives have some of the same trials and tribulations others go through. We are human. We just don't have the liberty to discuss with "our friends" what may be occurring in our lives. Our woes are compounded when you add the household duties and expectations with those of the church. Don't be so critical of the women standing behind the Pastor. You never know what is hiding under that hat.

Dr. Nina McGhee

"Even in the whispers and secret discussions, they gave us our space but made it clear – they didn't want anything to do with what we were doing."

ALL THE PREACHER'S WIVES
A Peek Behind The Curtain Of Being A Preacher's Wife

17
HINDSIGHT IS 20/20

After my 6-month hiatus, I walked into the sanctuary for Sunday School with Pastor and our three children. I hadn't even thought about the stares, side-eyes, or whispers that would occur upon my presence. Surely, someone would have something to say since I hadn't been at church for such a long time. Though I had conversed with many of the members during my MIA escapade, I did feel kind of anxious walking back inside of the church. To my surprise, it seemed as if I'd been there all the time. Well, that's for the ones who truly love. The devil was still present and still in full effect. The difference this time was that I did not care about their actions anymore.

Yes, First Lady stopped going to church with the family because I was sick of feeling like I did. Many times, it is easy for others to tell you how to feel or what you should do in given situations. Realistically, no one knows what they will do unless put in the same situation. Sunday after Sunday, I was tormented because two "Sisters" did all they could to make my Sunday worship experience with my family and church family a living Hell. Of course, I should have known that such happenings came with the "First Lady" territory. At that time, I did not want to PUSH (pray until something happens) through it. So, I gave up.

Leaving did not just happen. There were so many experiences that impacted my decision. It would take an entire novel to encompass the full story, which occurred in only a matter of months. It began with

ALL THE PREACHER'S WIVES
A Peek Behind The Curtain Of Being A Preacher's Wife

the smirk comments. Talking out of my presence and passing messages topped everything. On one occasion, Pastor was ill, and one of the "Sisters" had the nerve to bypass protocol and hospital policies to visit the emergency and hospital rooms. Looking back on that, I just shake my head. It really was not called for. At the time, I was furious. How could one be so disrespectful? Again, it comes with the territory. I am sure some have experienced even worse.

Ironically, this was not my first rodeo with women in the church. At a previous church where my husband pastored, a female member slipped some anonymous cards under the pastor's study door. I usually didn't go into the study first. This particular Sunday – I did. I instantly knew who the cards came from. I was extremely hot-headed then. There I go, prancing to the Sunday School classroom to call the young lady outside. She didn't move. From then on, it was all downhill with me and her. It was only a few years ago that I would speak to the lady. Again, I am shaking my head because that could have been handled differently.

Fast forward to our present assignment - I did give up the throne this time for a while. I was sick of it. I had feelings too. Therefore, I needed to find myself and what I wanted to accept or not accept. So, I quit going to church entirely. I don't think many of my family members or co-workers knew because I went along with my daily activities in the normal fashion. During the time that I was out, I moped around for the first month on Wednesdays and Sundays. Church was all that I knew from my youth. I didn't want to attend another church's services because I knew that would cause other unmerited conversations. Why is she here? Why isn't she with her family? I knew that it was taking a toll on my children. I would talk to them, but I still would not go to church. I really didn't care how Pastor felt. Still, I knew it affected him too.

I really felt that Pastor could alleviate the whole issue by speaking a word or words to put the congregants in their places. He would not. After realizing this, I had to put Nina in her place. Like I said, others always know what's best. I even thought that I knew what he should have done. I had to realize that I could only control me and my actions. Many times, that is hard to do, especially in the church realm. It is easy to find a scripture that fits your situation. Yet, the truth is the scripture was often given in a different context.

I would say that if he would have talked about how great I was or how much he loved me across the podium that things would have been better. Unfortunately, I have seen other pastors do that but would be cheating and lying the whole time. That is why it is very important to know who you are and whose you are.

From an early age, I wanted to be a pastor's wife – not for the recognition and dress-up moments. *(My mom always dressed me up for church, and I had received spotlight moments since elementary school. I was always at the top of my class and deemed – Homecoming Queen, Valedictorian… you name it.)* I wanted to be a pastor's wife because I just knew that pastors loved their wives like God loves the church. In addition, I so admired my First Lady growing up and the way her husband treated her. These two were leaders in my home church when I gave my life to Christ. So, I thought that pastors were perfect men, who loved their wives unconditionally and did no wrong. This was the ideal life. Living and learning really showed me the falsity of my thoughts. Now, I am sure that my pastor and his wife had their moments too. Still, their impact on me just goes to show others that impressions are very important. Your presentation to others should be in a fashion that pleases God. God wants his leaders to be real, but God doesn't want his leaders to show the negativity of servanthood. Some things just shouldn't be discussed with others, such as marital issues and family matters, unless one is teaching a lesson. Telling friends and family about personal issues will have others hating while you've forgiven and are back in love.

I met Pastor (my husband) one Sunday evening at a quartet singing in Alabama, where he was preaching. When he walked in, I asked my cousin, "Is that him?" Me being who I was back then was determined to be his "good thing." We dated. He wined and dined me. I thought he was the best thing since sliced bread (as people can say). There were some prior issues that Pastor and I encountered before getting married though. He was from a different state and had prior marriages and relationships. The same went for me – I had a prior marriage and prior relationships as well. He had children. I didn't. The children were never a problem in our relationship, but those prior relationships on his side took us through some twists and turns. If we had the communication line that we have now back then, things would have been smoother. It is true that one must live and learn.

When Pastor and I first got married, the issues kept piling up. He is a preacher who can deliver the Word extremely well. He can sing and "hoop." In the Baptist church, that equals a chick magnet. In addition to that, he is 15 years my senior. I thought nothing of that because I felt that the age difference was just a sign of his maturity. We had a lot in common, but there was no denying the age difference. Today, I just tell people that I keep him young. In our first year of marriage, I graduated from college, began my teaching career, and had our first son. Also, in our first year of marriage, we both could probably eat each other up one day and spit each other out the next.

Some of the greatest dilemmas in our marriage resulted from confidential conversations. My husband is an extremely caring person. He has a true heart for all people. Many times, people will try to take advantage of one's kindness. Noting that he is a pastor, and a lot of people seek pastors' advice, he would often talk to men and women about their problems. You know that there never was an issue with the conversations with the men. On the other hand, some of the confidential talks with women would not turn out too well once I found out about them. Some were sincere, and others were for attention. Still, most pastors have to hear people out.

For nearly the entire first decade of our marriage, we experienced trouble. He says that trouble sometimes comes with a suitcase meaning it's going to stay for a while. It did! I remember getting so mad numerous times and leaving with my oldest son. I left and stayed with a cousin in Nashville for two days and went right back home. The last time I ran away was after Hurricane Katrina. I had the bright idea of going to New Orleans with my oldest son. The bridge across Lake Pontchartrain was being repaired. I was so scared crossing the bridge that I said if I ever get back home, I'd never run again. To solidify that, a wise woman at a church where my husband pastored told me to never leave my home. I took her at her word. No matter what transpired after that, I wouldn't leave. He stayed off a few times, but I would remain at home mad thereafter. My mother would always tell me to keep my home together and do what the others couldn't. (She has been married to my dad for 67 years). Now, I know a wife can help build the home, but no one can change a man or woman from who they really are or desire to be. Only God can do that.

Pastor has always led flocks in the rural areas of Alabama and Mississippi. When I first started this First Lady business (LOL!), I would wear the (hot) suits and matching hats most of the time. Pastor and I would disagree with my hairstyles because I will do the braids and put various colors in. (I think he has gotten over that now.) I do see that some duos never "dress down." That's just not us. We really are not the traditional pastor and pastor's wife because he will go without a tie frequently, and that is A-Okay. Still, we always remember to be a reflection of God in our dress. Don't get me wrong, though. When it's time to look like royalty, we can put on a show. I just want others to know that it is acceptable to be yourself and not try to live up to the standards of others with your attire.

Pastors' wives often experience trust issues. It is hard to have friends because you never really know whom you can confide in. So, what is one to do? First and foremost, you have to trust God. After careful selection, you can sometimes find a few other pastors' wives who understand the joys and pains of the role. Also, there are a lot of clubs and organizations that are fitting for pastors' wives. You cannot keep everything bottled up inside. You have to free yourself, or you will go crazy, literally.

Yes, he is the pastor, and you are not. Still, if you sign up for the role, you have to live a set-apart life as well. Again, no one is perfect, but you should set limits to worldly indulgences. Pastors' wives cannot be clubbers or always in mess and havoc. That is not becoming in our profession. Profession? Of course, this work is a real J-O-B!

ALL THE PREACHER'S WIVES
A Peek Behind The Curtain Of Being A Preacher's Wife

We must support the Man of God. I have witnessed some pastors' wives realize that this work is not for them. I believe that if you want out and just cannot handle the role, get out. It is better to leave than to hurt the pastor, the church, others, and yourself. We all know what we can and cannot endure. Don't ever remain in a position because of what others expect. In the end, it is best to be realistic and to do what is best for the whole.

In addition, one must remember that only God knows the truth. When placed in certain situations, people will lie. Sometimes, the truth will prevail. Many times, the truth will hurt tremendously. I encourage all pastors' wives to stay prepared for life, in general. Life can bring some hurtful experiences. Then again, life can bring some joyful and amazing times that are unmatched. As a pastor's wife, one must be prayed up and willing to fight the good fight of faith. At the end of the day, somebody's gotta' do it.

When COVID-19 began to plague our lives, it brought my family closer together. We were stuck together for months. This taught me a valuable lesson. Spending quality time together can really pay off. During Spring 2020, my husband and I talked a lot about things that we had never discussed. Our children became more vocal with us as well. I can truly attest to the notion that communication is vital to any relationship. In the Summer of 2020, my mother became extremely ill and had triple bypass surgery. During this time, my marriage was on the rise. My husband and children pulled together to keep our home afloat while I spent lots of time caring for my mother. It seemed to be so easy. In prior instances, we would be bickering and quarreling. Yet, after our time to "come together," there was no stopping our team. I call us "The McGhee 5." I encourage First Families to have an intimate relationship with God and an unwavering communication line with each other. Talk about everything even if the conversations are uncomfortable ones. Work together as a team to overcome any and all obstacles.

Fast forward to 2022… After two pastoral tenures and now that the kinks are out, it is smooth sailing. I wouldn't dare say that we don't disagree or raise our voices at each other. Now, we just know how to approach any given situation. Know your limits. Set expectations initially and stick to them. Being a pastor's wife is a role of compromise. You cannot think that you will always be right. At times, even when you are right, you will have to bend. Being a pastor is a noble but time-consuming role. Thus, a pastor's wife must be understanding and creative in getting that time in. Time management is an important skill to master.

Know that family and friends will not always understand the role. Many family functions will be missed. Many family trips will not be on your agenda. For some, that can leave you feeling lonely and even depressed. Again, it comes with the territory. Still, there is a brighter side. One can find extreme joy in First Lady duties. I have always enjoyed supporting my husband. I have even driven him to church on Sundays and to revivals. The kids and I love the road trips. Sometimes, we just stay home and pray for Pastor. There is always a way to turn situations that appear trying into opportunities to help others.

Over the years, I have experienced some interesting happenings in the church. Church hurt can really take you to a place that you don't want to be in. At times, church folk can do some peculiar things. From wanting to let you hear them talking about your husband to telling you how to dress, you can encounter some frustrating situations. Ultimately, your response is everything. Thus, it is so important to pray daily for guidance and protection. Saying the wrong thing can cause a lot of future problems. I am not saying that you need to take anything and everything from parishioners. I am encouraging you to pray without ceasing and to pick your battles wisely. Above all, think before you speak.

When it comes to confidentiality, I insist that you use your Godly instincts. When church members confide in you, you must keep some things confidential. If you think that harm will be caused to someone, you need to seek the appropriate professionals. Otherwise, you are that shoulder for many members to call on and cry on. Some things you are told are best left inside. Often, the ladies in the church will look up to you and revere you as the leading lady. Therefore, it is

ALL THE PREACHER'S WIVES
A Peek Behind The Curtain Of Being A Preacher's Wife

extremely important to set a good example. I cannot emphasize enough how important it is to have a solid relationship with the Lord. Being a pastor's wife is not for the weak.

With all that transpires, remember to stay in your lane. The pastor is the pastor. His qualifications are noted in I Timothy 3 and referenced in other books of the Bible. The best advice that I can offer is that pastors' wives be supportive of their husbands. In addition, serving in the church in a God-led ministry is beneficial to oneself and the whole body of Christ. I am a choir member, assistant Sunday School superintendent, and program committee chairperson. I insist that you choose your auxiliaries and do not take on any duties that you know you cannot fulfill.

There are no manuals to the First Lady position. Truthfully, there are no set rules for handling any given situation as a pastor's wife. What works for one can be the detriment of another. Only God can help a woman in this role. Having a strong prayer life and an intimate relationship with God has proven to be the best route to fulfilling the position successfully. This role for me was purposed. It took me about 15 years to learn to live and to let live as a pastor's wife. It can be accomplished sooner if you move self out of the way. I know that I would have experienced many of life's challenges as a mere wife, but a pastor's wife must be a very unique woman because the challenges come at another level of intensity.

A few years into the journey, I deemed myself as "Only Lady" not First Lady or Elect Lady. It was not to make myself appear better than others. I just didn't want to fall into preconceived notions about pastors' wives. Though some might think you are not the only one, remember, you have to do what works best for you. At the end of the day, I have learned that this role is a great work. It is also a noble work. Everyone is not cut out for the job. Remember to protect your peace by any and all means necessary. Try not to lose yourself in being whom you do not want to be. If it is destined, it will come naturally. In regard to me, sometimes, you get what you ask for. Reflecting on it all, I could not have asked for anything better than being a pastor's wife.

Andrea "Shay" Gray

"Everything that I believed in the Word of God, everything that I taught from the Word of God, and everything that I practiced before the people of God were erased from my heart, mind, body, and soul."

ALL THE PREACHER'S WIVES
A Peek Behind The Curtain Of Being A Preacher's Wife

18
FROM BROKEN TO BLESSED

PRAISES TO GOD for this opportunity to share publicly my journey as a preacher's wife. I have been the wife of two preachers. I was so embarrassed about this status. I know what the scripture SAYS, but I was that guilty one that did not always ACT on what the Bible says. I KNEW scripture but I was not always the BELIEVER following God's plan.

I took a step back and did some self-inventory on myself after my 2nd marriage to a preacher. My mask is OFF!!

WHERE DO I START…. I think about my life growing up as a pre-teen and teenager in the Dallas Independent School District. I was always a little shy because I worried about how other students perceived me. I was already known as the "church girl" in my neighborhood – my parents were loving people and known in the community. My mother worked in the Dallas ISD school and retired. My dad worked for DART Rapid Transit until his health failed – he drove the Dallas city bus. Although my family was what they label as middle class in the 70's and 80's, I had some personal issues that I did not realize until I reached adulthood.

Perhaps if my "down days" had been diagnosed as depression early, I may have been a better ME! Because my past was not addressed, I went through two marriages. Growing up in church all my life, I was not surprised I was drawn to preachers. I was drawn to the suited and booted look, and of course, a man that could teach the Word was appealing.

My first marriage was based on church tradition – if you live together, you must marry because the bed is honorable and the bed undefiled…so we got married and had two beautiful children - a daughter and a son. It was wonderful to experience all the fun of planning a wedding, planning a baby shower, then having healthy babies! I felt tremendously blessed! However, the love was not there – I'm referring to me. I did not love my first husband. I loved what we had, but not the unconditional love. I played my role. I submitted to my husband and did what he asked of me. That is what a good wife does right? Well, this led to resentment among other things - which led to a divorce – no drama. The marriage was just over. I believe I was struggling with undiagnosed DEPRESSION and ANXIETY. Some days I felt like it was only the spirit of GRACE and MERCY that has gotten me through the journey of my first marriage of being a preacher's wife.

Then God blessed me with a chance to remarry. This time I knew I was in love. Then came joy and peace because this was my high school sweetheart that came back in my life. There were no plans to reunite from high school. How in the world did this happen? We couldn't put it together. We finally decided it was all God – GOD reunited us again after 20 years.

A week before our wedding, my new husband announced to the church he was called to preach. I was speechless but not surprised since he was a teacher by nature. I admit I was somewhat nervous, and people would tease me and say, "another preacher." Help Lord. I would smile and be OK with that because this man here stole my heart in high school.

At this time, I have many titles now. I am remarried and the mother of five bonus children and I had custody of my two biological children. All our children were close in age. At one point we had six of the seven children living with us. I was always adjusting because I wanted the husband and the children comfortable no matter what it took. I felt they were all my priority and I felt that I could fix anything. I would make calendars of the month with dinner already planned out. I had kitchen duties mapped out for each of the children as well on a calendar. I had everything organized in the home. I enjoyed these activities. It was hard for me to let the children grow up. I would find myself going behind them to clean up. My only rule was to make sure the bedrooms and bathrooms were always neat. They did ok, but instead of teaching them or correcting them, I would just fix things and keep it moving. I became the Fixer Mom.

As the children grew older, it became more challenging to be a wife, mother, and preacher's wife, and I was still a career woman. I was juggling all of these hats! And they were flying off and on like crazy! As life progressed, my husband wanted to start his own church. We started having church with all our children in our home. We used Romans 6:4 as our theme scripture. Later we were blessed to have a church building, a stranger came and pointed out that Romans 6:4 was also our wedding anniversary – June 4th. I was like "wow." I never saw it that way. We were amazed. We never saw the visitor again. This theme scripture still sticks with me today. The marriage ended because I allowed my emotions to take over. Everything that I believed in the Word of God, everything that I taught from the Word of God, and everything that I practiced before the people of God was erased from my heart, mind, body, and soul. I left because I felt my husband did not appreciate me. I know he did but when I left that was too devastating. I felt the children were disrespectful. I know they were getting older, but I wanted them to still abide by our house rules. I did not feel I was getting the support I needed from my husband to enforce the rules.

If you can tell by now the devil was all in the picture. No praying. No fasting. When the children were smaller, we would have family time. That was stripped. It was replaced with sports, long hours at work, and young adults having jobs of their own. I knew the family was not as close because of schedules but this goes back to my pre-teen and teenage days, that same fear muzzled my mouth. I wanted everyone happy, but I was not happy about the situation I was seeing. So, I tried to fix it. After all, I am the super organized Fixer Mom. I could fix anything…so I thought. I designed special family dinners so we could all sit around the table. And of course, many special occasions had to be commemorated by taking family pictures with all of our outfits coordinated. Family trips were also a part of my strategy. They included a trip to North Carolina, a Carnival Cruise to Mexico, and a flight to Mexico. I tried my own way and failed in so many ways. I lost the love of my life. I lost the bonding relationship with my biological children and my bonus children. I encourage anyone reading this section to seek God seriously and never stop praying. Never leave the home that you helped to build. Be wise and seek Godly counsel as well. You may be on the verge of giving up – DON'T DO IT!

As a two-time divorcee, THROUGH PAIN I FINALLY UNDERSTAND MY PURPOSE…You know what they say – better late than never.

"I HAD TO KEEP ENCOURAGING MYSELF. IT'S GONNA GET BETTER – IT'S GOT TO BE BETTER…. BECAUSE GOD IS IN CONTROL!!!!" A popular song by Hezekiah Walker.

I kept saying this to myself as tears soaked my pillow for a couple of years. Eyeballs were swollen and red because the tears would not stop flowing. I begin to feel it in my heart; that it's going to get better because God is in control.

I was in denial about myself. I laughed at myself. I cried by myself.

I would even be sarcastic in conversation knowing I was hurting inside.

A lot transpired in my almost fifty years of life!

If I was to make a theme for MY TESTIMONY, it would be BROKEN TO BLESSED

Listen, MY FAVORITE LOVE MOVIE IS CALLED "LOVE AND BASKETBALL," starring Sanaa Lathan and Omar Epps. To give a visual of my life, I would split my journey up into four quarters just like the "Love and Basketball" movie.

PRE-GAME – BROKEN TO BLESSED...

I gave up a lot before I realized I was disturbed growing up in my neighborhood, especially with the clicks in school. I was "churchy." I grew up in the Church of God in Christ. This meant no pants and no makeup was allowed. I was able to attend the convocations "back in the day". I was very young, and I did not go for classes. I went to look at the boys from different states. I did this because growing up all I did was go to church – Sunday morning, Sunday night, and sometimes visiting churches for 3:00 PM services. Throughout the week we would have Tuesday night youth service and Friday night Service. My mother cleaned the church so that meant going to church on Saturdays to help clean.

I was teased for going to church so much, but it was cool. I was the popular church girl. My classmates would say things like "Her Daddy Crazy!" "She Got a Goat for a pet in her backyard!!!!!" These things were true. I laughed, I joked but deep inside the teasing was hurtful and embarrassing. I wonder how many other people are looking great but feeling horrible.

I did not have many boyfriends. I was too "wholesome," too "churchy," and too boujee. (As they say now.) I didn't go to many school events, except the MAIN ones: The Sadie Hawkings Dance, prom, school pep rallies, and some basketball and football games. I didn't have time for hardly anything else.

ALL THE PREACHER'S WIVES
A Peek Behind The Curtain Of Being A Preacher's Wife

As I stated earlier, I am not surprised I was married to preachers.

Back to my first quarter of life. I didn't like asking for money from my parents. I didn't like lectures. I already had to deal with the teasers from school. The last thing I wanted to hear was "No" to my requests for money to go to a sports game or hear my dad give his lecture and then give me the money I asked for in the first place. This goes to show I liked to do everything on my own. These thoughts would affect me even living the preacher's wife lifestyle.

For these reasons, I worked at M.E. Moses, a small five-and-dime store in the neighborhood. I worked, so that eliminated my chance to play sports long-term.

Speaking of sports. I loved basketball then and now. I tried out my senior year in high school and made the team. My mother was not too keen on me playing sports because I had to stay after school for practice and the bus got us home late. I liked basketball, but the uniforms were very suspect, and I was not comfortable with the shorts they provided us. I guess it was the churchy girl in me. The shorts were very short and tight. When I ran, I could feel the shorts rising up my thigh and I could not focus on the drills well. Also, the boys would be practicing in the next gym and would come by to see us girls practice. I was shy then, especially with these little shorts the school provided.

By working at the five-and-dime store, I could avoid the teasers, not be confronted, and make my own money. Even as a preacher's wife I found myself doing things to avoid confrontations with family, others in the ministry, and even my husband. As a preacher's wife, I wanted everyone happy and pleased. My thoughts about situations around me, and my beliefs about how things were handled around me did not matter to me (so I thought). All this time, I was mentally becoming stressed out. How I wish I was wiser during these times in my life. I now know that my thoughts matter – YOU matter. We have a voice. Find within yourself the strength to HANG

IN THERE! It's not worth losing everything you worked so hard for. This is my aftermath – my survival after the preacher's wife's lifestyle.

Still Q1– BROKEN TO BLESSED

I tithed off my gross, not my net. I was raised to always tithe and always have insurance on everything! I saved money and gave my mom a portion. I've never had a broke day in all the days of my life! I'm not bragging, just blessed.

As a preacher's wife there were two incomes, and those services were where the congregation blessed you as well. Now, it's just me. I'm so glad I remember my home training. Always give God his 10%. I wanted to do more so that is why I tithe off my gross and not the net. I desire gross blessings. I serve a BIG God.

BLESSED…. TRANSITION BEGIN TO HAPPEN – I say this because although I made mistakes, I always put God first when it came to finances. I BECAME INDEPENDENT.

Here I am in the first quarter of life. Married with two children; enjoying the fun times; planning a wedding in my 20's; birthed two healthy babies in my 20's. Whoo-hoo! I'm thinking I'm living my best life! Bought my first home from the savings stored up from M.E. Moses. I had a reliable car and a great job with benefits. I loved everything going on in this season.

No fancy car like the stereotype of preachers' wives. I had a simple four-door Toyota Corolla.

But all the fun times did not last. Quarter One concludes with yours truly getting divorced, having two children, and becoming a college mom because I needed more income. In my profession as a human resource professional, the more letters behind your name, the better your chances are to receive a higher pay grade.

Q2 - TRANSITION TO BROKENNESS

I focused on myself. I focused on my kids. I had bills to pay, and I needed to take better care of myself. I remained active in the church. I entered into Quarter Two remarried with a blended family and receiving my Bachelor's and Master's degrees in business management. Now I'm a dog lover. My fur baby Charity (full-breed boxer) lived indoors with us. This was my new season, new blessings!

I was singing, "I'm So Glad Trouble Don't Last Always" Song By Timothy Wright.

I have to admit I was happy being a fixer to others. I must admit that whatever my family wanted, if, in my power, it would be done. However, I forgot about myself in this season just like in quarter one.

SPIRITUALLY – I was the first lady and wore many hats including heading up the women's ministry, and youth ministry, being secretary, leading the church conferences, arranging for outings, coordinating events to fellowship outside the church, and hosting events inside the home.

Here I am yet again, Fixer Mom, trying so hard to fix family issues that I compromised my beliefs. In addition to that, my job also became extremely demanding, subtracting time from my family. I didn't take ANY time for myself. My priorities were all messed up.

Q3 - BROKEN YET BLESSED IN MY MESS!

Now, yours truly….divorced again! This was when I finally sought professional counseling. I never considered this option before, even though I briefly tried couples counseling. It is important to use the professionals God planted on this Earth for that purpose. Skilled professionals are available if you want help. Don't wait until it's too late.

IT'S OK NOT TO BE OK. I went through depression. As a preacher's wife, this was one of the most embarrassing times in my life. I felt like a failure. I was the First Lady. My life was not supposed to look like this. During my counseling, I was INTRODUCED TO VULNERABILITY. Brene Brown's YouTube videos on vulnerability were awesome! I still go to YouTube to listen to inspirational speakers. Old thoughts still creep up. I welcome reminders that help me remember to just be me, flaws and all.

My faith is now at its weakest. I felt so lost. I let my emotions take full control over my life. My heart had been infiltrated and I was living out of that pain. (Proverbs 4:32). I didn't feel like I could fix anything. I felt useless. Unloved. I did not want to fight for marriage, and I had the opportunity, but because of self-inflicted pain, I proceeded with the divorce. I completed the paperwork. I thought it was the best thing to do so that my husband could move on because I knew he was tired of me going back and forth, leaving home and then coming back. As I sit and think, this was the craziest idea I ever had! I am the organizer, the planner. I failed big time. I put on my big girl panties and owned up to my mistakes.

My children stopped communicating with me during the divorce. I cried every day for countless days. My lash extensions were falling out. (I blamed the lash technician for using cheap products and charging high dollars.). That's how bad my crying was at the time. I still cry, but not every day. But when I do cry, they are tears of joy and tears of deliverance from fear. Hallelujah!! They are tears of restored faith because I am free to be me! I can be vulnerable and share my story.

I AM BLESSED AND HIGHLY FAVORED BY GOD.

NO TITLE ATTACHED – JUST MY NAME "UNDREA LASHA GRAY"

I had to remind myself that our children belong to God! I had to put them in His hands.

To be misunderstood is the most heartbreaking feeling to have. Not only was I misunderstood by my soulmate, my spouse, but I was also misunderstood by my children. I had no desire to eat. I was not sleeping. The counselor recommended a natural over-the-counter pill called Valerian to help me stay asleep. You are talking about a preacher's wife going through the darkest deepest tunnel of life. I did not survive COVID. My marriage did not survive COVID. My close to six-figure job did not survive COVID. Through it all, I thank God COVID did not take my soul out!

I tried to handle things in my own way and on my timeline. This was my Sarai moment. (Genesis 16). I felt like I would help God out. In reality, I was getting in God's way. It led to disaster! "Self" caused me to leave my love, my church family, and separation from my children. Everything changed!

This was my BROKENESS…. TOUGH SEASON (TOUGH QUARTER).

Q4 - BRIGHT HORIZONS, NEW ME

Looking on the brighter side, I'm still standing. Imagine what Quarter Four will bring! This season is the NEW ME. Just ME being ME, doing what God has told me to do. This quarter is still being played out.

The pains experienced made me understand my purpose. I am to be a light you can see. A motivator. An encourager. A supporter. I am to explore entrepreneurship. I am to emulate Christ in everything I say and do. I'm walking out the familiar verse "Too much is given, much is required." I said, "Yes, Lord to my purpose."

My testimony is that I've gone from brokenness to blessed. It's getting better. Although it's been a tug-of-war, because of grace, mercy, joy, and peace, I'm still standing. Why??

Glad you asked. I'm refocused. I'm stronger. I'm wiser.

ALL THE PREACHER'S WIVES
A Peek Behind The Curtain Of Being A Preacher's Wife

Through my pain and TRUSTING IN GOD, I have regained strength from God and have taken my women's church ministry, Sisters With A Testimony (S.W.A.T.), and relaunched it to be a nonprofit organization registered by IRS under 501c3 known as IElevate, Inc. to help less fortunate and left out women and girls. We provide hygiene products. We host events as well to encourage and motivate women and children.

As a preacher's wife, I was also used to having a companion. I thought I was ready for COURTSHIP, but GOD said NOPE! I know this because during this last fourth quarter I FASTED AND PRAYED FOR CLARITY. God said nope loud and clear.

The Bible says, "Jesus is our REFUGE." He was just that and rescued me from what I thought was a perfect new beginning AGAIN! All praises to God that it was a smooth ending to a six-month relationship. No hard feelings. This is how I know it was God that worked this small hiccup out on my behalf.

This quarter is still in progress. Restoration is still in the making. Our plans are not God's plans. Seek God's word for clarity for whatever you need answers to. We all have a choice. Choose the right one – Jesus.

When I thought I would go lacking because there was only one income, God said no – I GOT YOU. When I thought no one would love me anymore, God said no – I GOT YOU. I'm still here because of brokenness – brokenness made me who I am today. My faith grew strong again! As long as I live, I pray, and I gain continuous strength daily. Joy and peace came when I let go and let God have his way in my life! When I stopped worrying about what people thought about me and my life as a preacher's wife, God began to open many doors.

I still classify myself as a woman with many hats, but this time I know my worth.

As an entrepreneur, professional woman, and motivational speaker, people are more respectful and want to engage with me because of my vulnerability and the fact that I am honest. My testimony remains BROKEN TO BLESSED…BECAUSE GOD IS IN CONTROL OF MY LIFE. I strayed away as a preacher's wife but thank God I am back on track.

As I close out this quarter and blow the whistle…My testimony is:

I have unwavering faith now – I know God and believe in him…there's a difference.

Unwavering faith means – I trust God with my life more than I trust myself.

I trust his timing…. although I slip and want him to hurry up.

I trust his decisions when I do not like them.

I love him when I don't understand why I still hurt sometimes.

I'm blessed through my brokenness - amen.

Gina Fields

"Even in the whispers and secret discussions, they gave us our space but made it clear – they didn't want anything to do with what we were doing."

ALL THE PREACHER'S WIVES
A Peek Behind The Curtain Of Being A Preacher's Wife

19
FROM SUNDAYS TO THE SABBATH DAY

From my early stages of life, I had been brought up to worship the Lord on Sunday I attribute my spiritual upbringing to my grandfather, Leon C. Green – a hardworking, caring, devout man who had dedicated 52 years of his life in service to his faith and church membership. During this time, I was facing some exasperating issues in my life. I had been raised in an unstable home environment by a mother who loved me but could not always provide for me the things I needed as a young child. She could only love me as she understood love, which left me feeling that I had to toughen up, not become a victim of the abuse she received and thus inflicted on others. So, I cherished the love I felt from my grandparents, and it was my grandfather who helped me to see what true love was, introducing me to my first love – JESUS.

However, this love of God was not enough for a young 19-year-old college student. I became a mother to a beautiful son, longing for the love I desired from his father. At this time, we were just parents, trying to figure things out, but we did not give up. I attempted to show him what I expected out of our lives, but we were just not on the same page. So, I decided a change was needed. To get me back to where I was, I needed to be willing to start over. Not with him, but with my environment. I wanted to be loved. I needed to feel God's love. In that place, there were just too many obstacles I had to face. What did I do, a mother of a young son? I stepped out on faith. I moved from Louisiana to Dallas. I trusted God. Little did I know how that trust would save my life.

After moving to a new place, with no family, I turned to the Bible and the understanding of my grandfather. God was still revealing things in my life and had sustained me in ways I could not see coming. I loved reading the Bible and could not believe just how much I missed it. I longed for a study group. Then my best friend, who convinced me to move to Dallas in the first place, told me "You should meet my cousin. She and her husband study the bible and know about some of the things you've been studying." What?! A bible study group with someone who can potentially answer more questions or expound on topics of interest? Sign me up!

My best friend's cousin was also a hairstylist who specialized in hair braiding. Ironically, I had a scheduled appointment to get my hair braided by her prior to knowing she and her husband had a bible study group. But little did I know how this one appointment to get my hair braided would be the catalyst to the biggest life-changing experience of my life!

My appointment was at 6 am on a Sunday. That's the time she gave me. As I thought to myself, "Wow, that's early," I proceeded to ask her, "Since I'm coming early in the morning would you like for me to bring you any breakfast?"

She replied, "No thank you, but if you bring something for you to eat, I ask that you don't bring any pork."

I thought to myself, "No pork." That was a specific yet interesting request. But hey, I was going into her home, therefore, I had no problem with respecting her wishes. The next morning, I arrived at her apartment as scheduled. Katrice opened the door and there stood a short and petite young lady with a round face and a very inviting spirit. Katrice was a military wife with 2 small children (1 toddler and a newborn), creative, free-spirited, and very talkative. After inviting me in, she immediately asked me, "So, when I told you not to bring any pork, what were your thoughts?" I was a little thrown off by her timing and straightforwardness, especially with this being our first-time meeting. Nonetheless, I was transparent in my answer," Well, the first thing that came to mind was that you must be of the Muslim faith." Those were the only group of people I knew that did not eat pork. She laughed and said, "Yeah, we get that a lot!" She then asked, "So do you want to know why we don't eat pork?" As I looked at the clock above her TV, I thought to myself, I've been here 45 mins and we haven't started on my hair yet... but I replied, "Sure, why don't you?"

Katrice opened her bible and gave it to me to read as she began to explain to me the Lord's Dietary Law. I was blown away! "The Lord has a diet plan?!" Me being the health and fitness enthusiast I was and still am, this information was GOLD! She then began to take me through the scriptures showing me refutable beliefs based on what I had customarily practiced in the Baptist faith I grew up in. One is Sunday worship vs. the Lord's seventh day Sabbath. We read **Genesis 2: 1-5 and Exodus 20: 1-11 KJV** then afterward, went to the encyclopedia and looked up **Saturday vs. Sunday**, the definitions were clear, Sunday is the first day of the week and Saturday was the seventh day of the week, a day of rest and religious observance. But I always knew Sunday was the start of the new week, however, what I did not know was the Lord set aside (sanctified) a specific day (the 7th day) and hollowed it (made holy)! As I sat there awestruck but hungry for more information, what once was a hair appointment turned out to be a bible study, history lesson, and eventually a 24-year sistership. What I had been searching for that night as I sat on the floor of that empty bedroom wondering what I was going to do next; I truly believe the Lord wanted me to know through my encounter with Katrice – "You prayed for a new beginning – this is it, start NOW! - God"

ALL THE PREACHER'S WIVES
A Peek Behind The Curtain Of Being A Preacher's Wife

As for Me and My House, We will Serve the Lord – PERIOD!

And if it seems evil unto you to serve the Lord, choose you this day whom ye will serve……but as for me and my house, we will serve the Lord. Joshua 24:15 KJV

I am for the most part a very decisive person. I don't live in the grey, I am either black or white. Either I will or I won't. Either I'm all in or I'm out. Giving my all is the rule, NOT an exception. Therefore, a person will always know where I stand or where they stand with me. I will never forget reading for the first time (with understanding) the scripture, **Revelation 3: 15-16 KJV**, when the Lord says, "*I know thy works, that thou art neither cold nor hot: I would thou wert cold or hot. So then because thou art lukewarm, and neither cold nor hot, I will spue thee out of my mouth.*" Reading this was my Ah-ha moment! This scripture supports my approach to decision-making! Where others may look at this approach as "not being flexible", I (and the LORD) look at decision-making as definitive. It's important that when we make important decisions in life, we must gather ALL the facts, and consider perspectives to gain better insight to make informed definitive decisions. Why? For starters, it's what the Lord requires of us. Secondly, once your decision is made, you can stand in your decision being fully persuaded and confident.

I started with this backstory, so that you can understand, how after few months of studying the bible and doing extensive research with Katrice and my newfound bible study group, why I came to the decision to serve the Lord in Spirit and in Truth, which included, making the decision to change from worshipping on Sunday to keeping and honoring the Lord's seventh-day Sabbath. Once my mind was made up (on a Wednesday to be exact), I went "cold turkey" and started honoring the Sabbath to the best of my ability. No more going out on Friday nights, no more going to the mall, shopping, and hanging out on Saturdays. Instead, I was in bible study on Friday nights, and Saturday mornings, getting my son and me dressed to go to church.. It felt right, I felt good, and I wanted everyone I knew and loved to have this same feeling – Freedom in Christ and His Truth!

However, I would be remiss in sharing that this change was NOT easily accepted or adopted by my friends, family and nor my husband *(Yes, Glory to God! He finally made up his mind to move to Texas and we officially became a family!)* right away. Family and friends as usual, when you change your life for the better and from what they once knew you as, they are quick to ridicule you, especially when they don't fully understand the purpose behind your decision to change. This was the first challenge I faced.

As I continued to acquire my newfound knowledge, in Gina-like fashion with excitement and enthusiastic zeal, I started sharing what I was learning. First with my husband and my best friend (Katrice's cousin) of 30+ years, immediately I was told – "You do you, cause it ain't for me!" I didn't know if I was hurt or angry by their responses, maybe a little of both. All I remember is proclaiming, "This is my apartment (only because my name was on the lease), and I say, we will follow the Lord's Sabbath Day and His Dietary Law!" "That's right! No buying or eating pork or shellfish, etc.!" I will never forget the look they all gave me. You know the look, that "FIRST OF ALL" look you give someone who overstepped their boundaries. If I could read their minds that day, their looks were saying, "Really? First off, we are from Louisiana and second, we are grown, and we pay rent here too!" Yes, the zeal I had to serve the Lord as He commanded was not being exercised properly. In my young adult years, I didn't understand the importance of the Fruit of the Spirit when witnessing and evangelizing to people. I didn't understand that winning a person over to Christ is not by your conversation, but by your actions and submission to His Will. This would be a hard test for me, especially coming from a background of women whom I hadn't seen demonstrate humbleness and submission. My actions caused a response from my husband and best friend (she and her fiancé were our roommates) that would not only test my commitment to my new faith journey but also humble me in a way that was necessary for my personal and spiritual growth. The next day, after I 'put my foot down',I decided to go home on my lunch break to eat lunch *(it's important to note that this was not customary as I either ate at work or went out to lunch with co-workers* and in hindsight, I believe it was the Holy Spirit who moved me to this decision).. When I walked in, low and behold, there was a Louisiana feast taking place! Everyone was in shock, with eyes wide open, stopped what they were doing, and awaited my response. There they were, my best friend (who was a great cook by the way), her fiancé, AND my husband were frying up all the Louisiana favorites – you name it, they were cooking and eating it. At that moment, my eyes began to fill with tears, and I heard a still, small voice say, "Don't say a word, Gina." Although hurt by what I saw, I held my peace, got my lunch ready, and left to head back to work. On my way back to work, I called Katrice crying and asking, "Why are they making a mockery of me? Why outright disrespect me and the Lord this way?!" After trying to console me, she then recommended I contact the Sr. Pastor of our church, to seek Godly counsel on my situation. "Call the Pastor directly?!" Where I'm from, general members did not have direct access to the Pastor, you went through other channels – not him! Nevertheless, I took heed to her direction.

I took an extended lunch and called our Sr. Pastor (who had an open-door/call policy, and still does 25 years later). I told him my situation and what recently took place, thinking he would side with me and encourage me to go back and put my foot down harder. He said to me, and I quote, "Darlin' if your husband wants pork chops or anything else, you cook it or let him cook it, you just don't eat it!" As I held the phone speechless, I thought to myself "Wait! What? You want me to cook what? Doesn't this goes against God's law?" As he began to expound and explain, he shared the following scripture with me: "...*If any brother hath a wife that believeth not, and she be pleased to dwell with him, let him not put her away.* **And the woman which hath an husband that believeth not**, and **if he be pleased to dwell with her, let her not leave him. For the <u>unbelieving husband is sanctified by the wife</u>**, and *the unbelieving wife is sanctified by the husband...*" 1 Corinthians 7: 12-14 KJV.

What this scripture and counsel taught me, was the importance of getting The Lord's Truth for me first! I must study to show myself approved. Let the Word of God transform me and prayerfully, through my obedience my husband too will be sanctified! The humility and hope I received through that scripture set me on the path of spiritual focus and transformation.

Transformation starts with the Renewing of the Mind

And be not conformed to this world: but be ye transformed by the renewing of your mind, that ye may prove what is that good, and acceptable, and perfect, will of God. Romans 12:12 KJV

Our family is growing, I am now pregnant with our second child – a girl! Being pregnant with my daughter was a big deal for me. I believed the Lord was blessing me with an opportunity to correct my past wrongs through her. Not helicopter parenting but instead hyper-focused on raising a righteous seed unto the Lord. My husband and I decided it was time to part our separate ways from my best friend and her fiancé and move into a place of our own without distractions.

At this juncture in my faith journey, it had been several months since I took heed to the Godly counsel I received from my Sr. Pastor, I had been focusing on my transformation only, leaving my husband alone and at peace. It's Friday night, and I started the Sabbath off with an amazing bible study with my church study group! Upon returning home, I immediately got my son and I showered, and clothes prepared for church the next day. My husband is home, watching the Mavericks vs. Lakers basketball game in the bedroom. As I got in bed, I decided to review my bible study notes and re-read some scriptures. He didn't say anything to me as he knows by now and respects that I am "honoring the Sabbath." However, out of my peripheral, I noticed him sneaking glances over at me. After a few minutes of him waiting for me to notice him, he proceeds to ask me, "So, what are you reading?" I paused before answering because I could not believe he was inquiring! This was the first time he showed interest in what I was studying. After I got over the initial shock, I proceeded to read and explain Hebrews the tenth chapter. I could not believe I was able to explain the scripture plainly and build on its precepts. I had only studied this passage earlier that night. After I concluded, my husband said, "You were able to get all of that you just said from that one passage, and you learned this in bible study?" In amazement, I said, "Yes!". Before going to sleep, I thanked the Lord for that space in time where I was able to engage in the Word of God with my husband, that we have more opportunities to study together, and he continues to be receptive. The next morning was different from every other Sabbath, I woke up to start getting my son and me ready for church, when suddenly, my husband says to me, "I'm going with you today." In shock, I responded, "To CHURCH?!" He said, "Yes." Our son was so happy, he said "Yay! Daddy's coming with us!" As I fought back tears; I sent up another prayer of Thanks to the Lord! From that day forward, he attended bible studies and church with us every Sabbath without fail for the next 24 years and counting.

Here I am, a living witness to the scripture that was read to me 9 months prior, "**For the <u>unbelieving husband is sanctified by the wife</u>….**" and just as the scripture prophesied, through my obedience to the scripture, my husband was sanctified!

Mountains and Valleys – Part 1

Blessed are ye, when men shall **revile you**, and **persecute you**, and shall **say all manner of evil against you falsely**, for my sake. **Rejoice, and be exceeding glad: for great is your reward in heaven:** for so persecuted they the prophets which were before you. Matthew 5: 11-12 KJV

ALL THE PREACHER'S WIVES
A Peek Behind The Curtain Of Being A Preacher's Wife

Fast forward a few years, and a lot has happened. Our families and friends are discussing our "weird beliefs". Worshipping on Saturday, ok, that's something they could align with a belief system they knew of – Seventh Day Adventists (SDA). But no, we're not of the SDA faith either. Some even questioned if we were in a cult! What else would explain why we no longer celebrated holidays but instead celebrated the holy days as outlined in Leviticus 23rd chapter of the Bible? Our going to church on Saturdays was one thing but not celebrating Christmas, Easter, etc.?! "Yeah, they must be in a cult." Come on now! If they truly knew me…knew us, they would've known this **was not** the case.

My family thought maybe it was a phase I was going through. Because as my mother put it, "Girl, please! What do you mean you don't celebrate holidays anymore? You grew up with Santa Claus and the Easter Bunny!" My husband's family believed that he was just following me. Not knowing that he was fully capable of studying the bible and rightly dividing the Word of Truth for himself. Even in the whispers and secret discussions, they gave us our space but made it clear – they "didn't want anything to do with what we were doing."

So, here we stand, my husband and I serving the Lord and His church **together**! Won't He do it?! My husband is leading the Evangelism team and Tape-recording ministry, recording all of the bible messages of our resident and traveling ministers of the church. (Yes, tapes! Before Audio Visual ministry was broadly adopted) and me, well, with our local congregation being under 50 members at the time, I took the initiative, as I'm accustomed to doing, to start volunteer lists for ministries that I was accustomed to seeing and being a part of in church that I thought would be beneficial to my new church home! Almost half of our congregation were children. Children = a need for a children's class. The church hosted and celebrated the Lord's annual holy days which included members cooking and serving foods, which means we needed menu coordination and assignment of tasks. We always opened with a reading of a Psalm before the minister would start his message. No singing, just a reading of scripture. I grew up singing

ALL THE PREACHER'S WIVES
A Peek Behind The Curtain Of Being A Preacher's Wife

in church and school choirs, but my new church did not have a choir. Music was a missing element in our church. I grew up knowing music was one way to usher in the Holy Spirit. Music sets the tone for the minister and his delivery of God's message. So, no choir = Choir signups. We needed a single source outlet that would allow us to stay abreast of world events, provide biblical inspiration, and keep us up to date on local church events and news (this is before social media platforms). A single source outlet = a Church newsletter, The Four Winds was born!

These all seem like great initiatives for a growing church, right? Well, one would think so. Unfortunately, I was met with opposition on all fronts. Sisters in the church felt I was going too far. "Who does she think she is", they said. They argued I was trying to "force" them to participate by putting up sign-up sheets. "Who told me I should be the one initiating?" They contested that there needed to be "a man heading up these initiatives, not a woman." I didn't get it. I was just in their good graces' weeks prior! These initiatives are great things for our church to have. Why is there an issue? Even Katrice became a part of the mutiny.. Katrice. Really?

After a few more years of progressive organizational attempts and being shut down each time only for other people to step in, pick up where I started, and then it's accepted; I had become weary. My husband and children saw me crying at home, saying, "I did not want to return to THAT church!" My husband tried to get me to realize, "Gina, you're not going to church for them. This is your commitment to the Lord!" Then to hear my daughter who was 9 years old at the time, tell me, "Mommy, you're not going to church? Don't you love God?" From the mouth of babes, her words convicted me more than what anyone else could have said. Remember, when I was pregnant with her, I believed the Lord blessed me to have a daughter to correct my past wrongs. And here I am demonstrating a poor example of a servant of God! That self-same day I got up and went to church and have not missed a day since (with exception of illness). I will say, I did not return with the upbeat, welcoming and servant enthusiasm I once had. Nope, I don't trust anyone now. Therefore, the silent treatment and distance were the best I could give at that moment. After all, isn't this the Gina they wanted?

Over the years to come, I would eventually find myself and my way back to doing what I love most, serving the Lord and His church. I was able to do so by remembering my daughter's resounding words "Mommy, don't you love God?". Yes, my love for the Lord, my family and giving them the best example possible are the reasons I continue… But my heart to serve the Lord knew nothing of the mountains and valleys that lay before us!

Mountains and Valleys – Part 2

After suffering a major loss in membership over disagreements in doctrine, leadership, and mishandling of membership, the church finally entered a season of 'peace' and was growing again! Some former members returned. Church family bonds were being forged. We started seeing spiritual growth in our local pastor, Bro. Mitchel. He finally established a leadership team that included my husband and I and several other 'pillars of the church' and we all started working together towards a common goal - revisioning and rebuilding our church's future. Based on my background in organizational and program management, I was assigned to coordinate our Church Reorganization project. After numerous meetings, late-night brainstorming, defining, and formalizing an organizational structure for ministries and committees for our church branch. Our church leaders are now ready to present changes to the church body and start implementation – but wait! Yes, you guessed it. Opposition met us before the first change could be presented.

Our metaphorical "7 years of plenty" (aka time of peace) was over! We were faced with a barrage of everything that was wrong with the organizational structure even though we built many policies and procedures based on their feedback. What stood out the most was a comment from one of the sisters, and I quote, "I'm not following any process or procedure, that was developed in McKinney!" This statement was made because it was known I was working with the Bro-Pastor Mitchel, his Elders, and leadership on the church reorganization project AND because I live in McKinney, TX. Here we go again! I will spare the details, but let's just say I failed at exercising the Fruit of the Spirit that day. With all the hard work and effort put into the project, only to hear complaints without solutions coupled with blatant disrespect, I was outdone. We knew what would soon follow, disgruntled members calling our most Sr. Pastor of our church organization (remember he has an open door/call policy), complaining about what's going on at the local level limited information, and mixed with untruths. How can our most Sr. Pastor make an informed decision with being ill-informed? He can't and how fair is that to him?! This type of breach in the spirit and unacceptable behavior from disgruntled members causes a strain on local leadership and dampens the morale of forward progress as well as sows discord among brethren – just one of the many things the Lord hates.

Eventually, we would implement the reorganization plans, but it would literally take us 7 years (aka 7 years of famine) to fully implement and gain the buy-in from the members. During these '7 years of famine', our beloved pastor Bro. Mitchel was removed from his post due to an indiscretion and my husband was asked to be his replacement – an invitation my husband quickly declined and recommended another Elder to stand in his stead. Bro. Garrison immediately accepted the position, and just like that, we are now under new leadership. With Bro. Garrison as our new local pastor, there wasn't much of an adjustment because he ministered in the same spirit as Bro. Mitchel, but his pastoral leadership was that of calm and decisive spirit. Leadership that my husband and I greatly admired and appreciated. Under Pastor Garrison's leadership, we experienced more church growth and just as in previous periods of growth, came fiery darts of opposition.

Another mutiny arose, but this one had to be the worst of them all! They planned, preyed, and plotted various attempts to get specifically Pastor Garrison, me, and my husband (a man that's liked and gets along with everyone) removed from our leadership roles. The insurrectionists wrote letters to our most Sr. Pastor and went as far as catching a flight to our church headquarters to have a meeting with him. During that meeting, they corroborated to **revile**, **persecute**, and say all **manner of evil against us falsely.** And in their prideful lust, they requested that they be added to the Pastoral leadership office to "ensure proper order just how church headquarters would have it." Their requests were granted, and three elders were added to Pastor Garrison's Elder Board without him, or my husband having a chance to defend themselves or rebuttal the decision made.

No Weapon Formed Shall Prosper

***No weapon** that is **formed** against thee **shall prosper, and every tongue that shall rise against thee in judgment thou shalt condemn.** This is the heritage of the servants of the Lord, and their righteousness is of me, saith the Lord.* Isaiah 54:17 KJV

As my husband says, "the Lord never said weapons would not form, He said they wouldn't prosper!" After the decision was made to add the three new additional elders, the following Sabbath I was called into the office by Pastor Garrison and my husband. They sat me down and shared with me the changes that were being made to leadership and how it all came to fruition. Afterward, they revealed what was said in the meeting at headquarters and that it was requested that I step down from serving in the Youth church and if I continued to direct the adult choir, I could not make any announcements on the mic or exhort the people to worship and praise. Well Lord, what type of weapon is this? It's formed and it appeared it has just prospered by hitting me in my chest hard! After I cried and pleaded with them both. I stood my ground on the fact, that *(1) the process of handling an 'ought' with your fellow brother or sister as outlined in* ***Matthew 18: 15-17 KJV*** *was not followed; and (2) this decision was made off falsehoods and therefore I shall not be moved!* No longer could I allow myself to be bullied by spiritual wickedness in high places whose goal to quench my spirit has been made apparent. I am tired of fading in the shadows to satisfy their fleshly egos and insecurities. After I respectfully spoke my peace, my husband and Pastor Garrison dismissed me, and I humbly went back to my regularly scheduled program of servitude.

The infiltration of the church leadership team consistently wreaked havoc, stirring up strife and discord within the church. My husband and I made the decision to lay low, stay focused on the Word of God, keep serving the Lord and the church, remain prayerful, patient and trust that the Lord will eventually vindicate us.

The Patience of the Saints – Pray. Wait. Trust.

*Here is **the patience of the saints**: here are they that **keep the commandments of God, and the faith of Jesus**.* Revelation 14: 2 KJV

Through all that my family and I had gone through with being servants of God, and in service to His church and His people, I am reminded of the parable of the Sower, specifically **Matthew 13:24-20; 36-43 KJV**. Here Jesus explains the necessity of allowing the wheat (sons/children of God) to grow with the tares (children of the wicked one) and how at the harvest (in the end) they both will receive their just reward.

Lord knows, I have been patient. I have consciously taken the bumps and bruises I've experienced along my faith journey whether I caused them or they were unwarranted and made several adjustments to my Woman of God profile. I finally began to understand that the Lord was taking me through these trials of fire to humble and refine me for something greater! As I allowed the Lord to use me, I prayed to the Lord to mature me in the Fruit of the Spirit, to give me a keener spirit of discernment, and groom me into the Woman of God He would have me to be for Him and my husband. And the Lord did and continues to do just that! In my patience, the Lord has shown me that "sometimes the greatest test we will receive as a servant is how we quietly handle those who so boldly mishandle us"- **Luke 6:27-38 KJV** and that perfect peace awaits us if just stay focused and trust in Him and His Word - **Isaiah 26: 3 KJV.** My husband always says, "when you pray for something (i.e., patience, temperance, etc.) be prepared because you'll never know how the Lord will choose to manifest that fruit in you." This is the truth and a lesson well learned!

It's official our prayers have been answered! With the record growth of our congregation, we've purchased our new church home and have started moving into our new space. With our first Sabbath Day service scheduled for January 6, 2018, I had made plans on Sunday, December 17, 2017, to host choir rehearsal at the new church location and to do a video recording of one of our original songs "If You Love God." We were all present, including Pastor Garrison because prior to being appointed pastor, he was one of our original Voices of Zion choir members and he loved to sing! We rehearsed as planned and Pastor Garrison did a round of mic checks on our AV system, prepping for his first message in the new church. Afterward, he complained about being tired and experiencing arm and leg pain over the weekend and was going to go home and take a nap. After we all left the church, I couldn't stop thinking about this new journey our congregation was about to embark upon and how it would impact our church's future.

I arrived home just in time to assist my husband as he gets ready to leave for work. He had been with his company for 25 years at this time, working nights from Sunday – Thursday. This night, as I was reviewing the video from our choir rehearsal earlier that day, the thought came to my mind once again about the future of our church. I was not sure why this thought kept coming to me but as I laid down that evening to go to sleep, I received a vision. My husband was standing behind a podium in an unfamiliar building. Another vision came to me, and he was catching a plane with his bible in his hand. I immediately got up. It was almost 4 am, the time he usually arrives home from work. So, I went into the kitchen and sat at the kitchen island waiting for him to walk through the garage door. At 4:05 am, he walks through the door, we greet each other, and I begin to fix his dinner. He wanted to know what I was doing up and I told him I couldn't sleep and that the Lord kept sending me visions. After he inquired, I began to tell him my visions. I proceeded to ask him, "Have you thought about preparing lessons to teach (lessons are equivalent to sermons)?" "What if Pastor Garrison, starts traveling to some of the other church locations, don't you think you should probably prepare to intercede in his absence?" "What if the Lord is showing me that you will become head pastor from headquarters!" He quickly stopped me and said, "I don't think the Lord was showing you that!" We both laughed but he agreed that the Lord had placed on his thoughts as well him to start working on a lesson/message he would teach. He shared some of his reservations with me that night, I then encouraged and reminded him of this fact, "The Lord *will give you what you need and words to say to give to His people, just like He gave Moses, Aaron who was eloquent in speech. Just pray and trust that the Lord will provide for you too!"* We both went to bed with minds racing about the possibilities.

At 4:50 am our sleep was interrupted by a phone call from Pastor Garrison's wife. When she woke that morning, she discovered him unresponsive. Regretfully, he passed away in his sleep. How could this happen? I was just with him the day prior! We had so many things planned. I couldn't think more of that now. My husband and I jumped-up, put-on clothes and headed to be at Sis. Garrison's side.

Be Strong and of Good Courage – I Am with You!

Now after the death of Moses the servant of the Lord it came to pass, that the Lord spake unto Joshua the son of Nun, Moses' minister, saying, **there shall not any man be able to stand before thee all the days of thy life: as I was with Moses, so I will be with thee: I will not fail thee, nor forsake thee. Be strong and of a good courage:** *for unto this people shalt thou divide for an inheritance the land, which I swore unto their fathers to give them. Only be thou strong and very courageous, that thou mayest* **observe to do according to all the law, which Moses my servant commanded thee: turn not from it to the right hand or to the left, that thou mayest prosper withersoever thou goest.** Joshua 1: 1, 5-7 KJV

ALL THE PREACHER'S WIVES
A Peek Behind The Curtain Of Being A Preacher's Wife

After the untimely death of Pastor Garrison, my husband receives a call from our most Sr. Pastor. "Troy," he says, "I need you; I need you to lead the church down there." My husband, just as he had felt times before, did not want the position. He saw firsthand, the stress and pressure the people put on those in leadership positions, especially the pastor! He knew he was not the man for the job. As he told Bro. Garrison, "you pastor the church, and I'll run the operations." That's what my husband did well, logistical operations. He did it in his professional life and now for the church. Nevertheless, my husband agreed to "think about the invitation and follow up with our Sr. Pastor later."

Later that evening, my husband came to me and asked what my thoughts were regarding him accepting the position as Pastor. I answered his question with the question, "How do you feel about assuming the role?" He explained that he didn't know if he could deal with the people because he saw the stress it put on Bro. Mitchel and Bro. Garrison and didn't want to end up like them, stressed out. He was also concerned with what it would mean for our family. The fiery darts of opposition on us is one thing but this position would expose our children (whom we shielded from the attacks for the most part) to be targeted. Most importantly, the responsibility of pastoring is one thing, but teaching the Word of God to the people puts their road to salvation in your hands. My husband did not want to run the risk of teaching something in error and leading the people astray.

I listened to and empathized with my husband's concerns which were all valid, and after I processed what he was saying and what he wasn't saying, the Lord moved me to tell him, *"Don't you worry for nothing, everything we've been through up until this point the Lord was clearly preparing you...Us! Cast your cares on Him. In all the prophets, men, and women of God in the Bible, He never forsook those who served Him in Spirit and Truth. So why would he forsake you?! Remember what I said the other night, He will give you what you need to lead His people. Just pray and trust He will provide."* We prayed together at that moment. He later called our Sr. Pastor and told him that he would accept the position and that he was doing so because he did not want to leave our congregation in the hands of someone that did not know our church and our culture.

The well-being of the people in the church has always been a priority for my husband. A man that is known for his humbleness, his love for the Word of God, and his dedication to the church will prove to be just a few of the many attributes that would make him a great spiritual leader and the right man for the job! Did the opposition cease? No. After the appointment and announcement of my husband as pastor, the fiery darts of opposition were dialed up a notch. However, we stayed focused on our original commitment – we will wait on the Lord's vindication. And in the end, their weapons never did prosper after all.

I love Jesus. I love my husband. I love our church. But I don't always love being a Pastor's wife.

Now five years into Pastoral leadership, on the bright side, if there is such a thing, the attacks on my family did not stop, they just come in waves. There are periods of peace and then – out of the blue my husband is receiving a call from our most Sr. Pastor receiving a reprimand and/or defending me or a decision he made as the Pastor of our local church that disgruntled members did not agree with. And just like the concern my husband had early on, eventually, the fiery darts buffeted our children. When tares could not get to my husband, the first target was me (now the Pastor's wife) and now our children. From my daughter "teaching" the children's class (she was an assistant only) and she is told she could no longer serve to my son and his fiancé (now wife) getting pregnant prior to their scheduled wedding day and they both being removed from serving in the music ministry. When my children are hurt or being affected, the fiery darts take on a whole different kind of pain. However, I remain focused on my husband's charge and our commitment years ago because there's no greater joy than to see our children together in the church, and now seeing my son with his spouse and son, loving, and desiring to serve the Lord. I think our children are richer and wiser because of their exposure to their father and I's service in ministry and how we continue to preserve not matter obstacles we are faced with.

There are so many things over the years I wish our church congregation would have understood and would take into consideration about my life and now, the current position I'm in today. So, I kindly ask all who reads this anthology – family, friends, church members, church leadership, and aspiring pastors' wives: Take a moment to think about your pastor's wife. What expectations have you placed on her? What is she doing that you love? What does she do that is confusing? Has she hurt you? Because so often we look at the actions of the pastor's wife —How involved is she? What is she wearing? Where is she serving? Why does she sit during worship? Why doesn't she reach out to me? But w**hat if you considered <u>WHO she is</u> instead of WHAT she does or doesn't do?**

So, what can I say to those wondering what it is like to be a pastor's wife? First, being a pastor's wife is a high calling, a great responsibility and although not highlighted in my testimony, it is also a Blessing! I frequently think about the scripture *"For unto whomsoever much is given, of him shall be much required: and to whom men have committed much, of him, they will ask the more. Luke 12:48"* Therefore, it is a gift from God to be in this position that I am in, yes, even during the tough times. There are many demands, yet the joys far outweigh the pressures. Secondly, I'm continuing to learn so much more about myself after becoming a Pastor's wife. One of the major learnings is that I know who I am always in Christ and be focused on pleasing Him first and foremost. And finally, when dealing with the congregation, I've come to terms with I cannot please everyone. Because if you try, it will become your downfall.

Over me and my husband years in ministry together, including pre-Pastoral office years, God has taken our pain and loss and turned those ashes into something beautiful. He has remained faithful to His

ALL THE PREACHER'S WIVES
A Peek Behind The Curtain Of Being A Preacher's Wife

Word. Thus, we remain faithful. Above all else, I now know that, apart from God, I can do nothing without Him… *John 15:5 KJV* and I wouldn't trade my assignment as a pastor's wife for anything else.

Peace, Blessings & Favor to all who read, empathize, and understand!

Sis. Gina Fields

Jamie Haddock

"But where is an appropriate meeting spot for a female pastor to go on a date? What do I wear? Can a female pastor be sexy?"

ALL THE PREACHER'S WIVES
A Peek Behind The Curtain Of Being A Preacher's Wife

20
THE DATING GAME

Introduction: You've heard "All the Preachers' Wives" stories, but I'm here to offer another perspective. Although there are many stories, I can tell about the struggle of being a female pastor, let's focus on my dating drama. I've been single for almost five years now, with a few relationships scattered throughout those years, but for the most part, my dating life as a pastor has been a disaster.

It's that time of the year again, the end of summer and the progression into cooler weather and holiday celebrations. It is a time for Fall festivals, Thanksgiving, Christmas, ringing in the new year, and Valentine's Day. This time of the year, from October through February, is often referred to by many as the cuffing season. It's the time when single people who have been dreading the dating scene "suck it up" and get out there for the sake of not having to be alone through the holidays. For those who are perfectly happy being single, like myself, the common motivation for taking the initiative to date is that we can do it on our terms instead of idly sitting back while our family, friends,

ALL THE PREACHER'S WIVES
A Peek Behind The Curtain Of Being A Preacher's Wife

and even our congregants look for people to set us up with. I feel a sense of lingering dread because I know it's only a matter of time before people start asking about my dating life again. Sometimes when I'm asked who I'm dating, I tell them that Jesus and I are in a long-term relationship, and I'm married to the church. Unfortunately, that answer doesn't seem to deter people from trying to demonstrate their matchmaking skills.

Dating, for me, is complicated and frightening. I'm the senior pastor of a small rural congregation in an eastern North Carolina town of about 2500 people. When you live in a small town, most everyone knows each other or at least knows of each other, and people like to talk about who they know and what they know, or rather, what they think they know. Some people call it gossip, but that word isn't very appealing, so most people just refer to it as a "conversation." I've been the topic of a few "conversations" that I am aware of. Recently, I called a church member to tell her that our church had added her son to the prayer list. As our conversation shifted, she asked if it might be OK for her to ask me a question. I replied, "of course," to which she asked, "Did you recently get married?" I laughed and said, "No, I'm not even dating anyone." I'm not sure if she heard I got married or if she just had me confused with someone else. There have also been some wild and somewhat scandalous accusations around town concerning men that people think I'm secretly dating. I think these rumors begin as harmless conversations, but as with any conversation that might be considered juicy, it quickly escalates beyond recognition.

As a pastor, I am sometimes contacted by men who are not a part of my congregation. Oftentimes they do not have a church home and are just looking for a safe person and space to talk about various issues taking place in their lives. I usually invite them to meet me at a restaurant or in some public setting, although if they live in town, I have sat on the front porch of the parsonage talking with them. This is how the rumor starts: I'm seen talking to a man, and the next thing you know, people are planning my wedding or condemning my choices. Ok, maybe I'm exaggerating a little, but honestly, every time I meet a male colleague, friend, or someone who just needs to talk, I fear that these encounters might be misconstrued as dates or the formation of an intimate relationship.

Dating Drama:

I decided some time ago that it would be in my best interest not to date anyone in the town that I serve for various reasons. So, if I'm not going to meet someone in town, then how am I going to meet someone? Online? Do I really want someone to tell one of my church members that they saw my dating profile on Bumble? Granted, some would probably be excited that I'm putting myself out there, but others might not view online dating in such a positive light. Although it's lost a lot of its stigma, it is not seen by many as the desired platform for a woman in ministry to meet someone.

After sharing my dating drama with another female pastor at a retreat, she followed me back to my hotel room and excitedly helped me create an online dating profile while assuring me that this was a perfectly healthy way for a single female pastor to meet people. I matched with a few different people. If they were still interested in me after I told them that I'm divorced, have two kids, and help care for my mom, who lives with me, the conversation inevitably shifts to "What do you do for a living." When I reply that I am the pastor of a congregation, I typically get two different responses. The first is that I'm ghosted completely. I think this is because they are intimidated by an independent woman who leads her own household and a church, or maybe they don't like the idea of being involved with a pastor for other reasons. The second isn't intimidated, and hopefully, our conversations will lead to an in-person date. But where is an appropriate meeting spot for a female pastor to go on a date? What do I wear? Can a female pastor be sexy? Can I wear my spaghetti strap above-the-knee red dress with high heels, or do I need to pair the dress with a nice cardigan and flats? Is it acceptable for me to drink wine with my meal? Unfortunately, the answers to those questions can be radically different depending on who you ask.

ALL THE PREACHER'S WIVES
A Peek Behind The Curtain Of Being A Preacher's Wife

I actually met someone online and started dating him. As our relationship progressed, he began attending church with me and participating in various community events as well as church activities. I would say that our relationship was fairly typical to that of other people who date someone who works the second shift. He would get off work late and come to the church parsonage to spend time with me. Watching tv and eating late-night snacks had turned into just about the only time we could find to get together, given our opposing schedules. After seeing his car in the driveway late at night, someone speculated that he was staying overnight, which created some gossip, I mean conversations, within the town that later got back to me, letting me know that was inappropriate behavior for a pastor. Unfortunately, over time our schedules became too much for us to manage, along with other complications, so we mutually decided to end the relationship. The aftermath of my dating someone and including them in the ministry aspects of my life is that if the relationship doesn't work out and we break up, the break up is very public. People noticed that this person is no longer coming to church anymore or at church events with me or community activities which ultimately leads them to ask what happened to so-and-so, to which I have to reply we broke up.

Dating a pastor comes with many challenges and requires a high level of trust. I've had complications during relationships as a result of a male congregant calling me at various times in the evening hours because he was struggling with different situations in his life. He really needed counseling and pastoral care, and my partner at the time was not able to understand that, as a pastor, I don't have regular office hours. I have to be able to minister to congregants when they need me. Whether that means getting up in the middle of the night to go to the hospital, doing home visits, or taking phone calls or texts all hours of the day. There are times when certain boundaries have to be drawn to maintain a healthy balance in my personal life. It isn't easy figuring out when a boundary needs to be put in place, but that boundary has to be set by me, not by my partner, and it needs to be set for reasons other than my partner's mistrust or insecurities.

ALL THE PREACHER'S WIVES
A Peek Behind The Curtain Of Being A Preacher's Wife

I walk this very thin line between wanting to keep my dating life a secret because I don't want my relationship to come under scrutiny and also really wanting the person I'm dating to be a part of every aspect of my life. I want them to go to church and activities with me so that we can see how that goes. But I fear that if our relationship doesn't work and we break up, how hard that will be for me. It's hard enough to go through a breakup in private without the whole community knowing about it. It's difficult when I'm dating someone to decide when and if I bring them into the ministry part of my life because if the relationship ends, it's a very public thing. If I am dating someone, but I don't feel comfortable inviting them to church or church functions, there's a heightened interest in why this person isn't accompanying me. I have dated people who don't like church stuff or being part of community events. We like each other, and dating is going well but merging my personal life, and my public ministry life sometimes seems at odds with one another. One guy I was talking to was concerned that the requirements of publicly dating me went beyond coming to service on Sunday and different activities and expanded into a life of ministry. He had a good point because if you look at the lives of preachers' wives, they are very much a part of their husbands' ministry. Is that the same expectation if the pastor is female? That idea doesn't seem to be as desirable to a man dating a female pastor as it does to a woman who is dating a male pastor. When women meet men and discover they are pastors, there is an ideology about what kind of woman they will need to be to support the pastor in their ministry. That often includes becoming an agent of ministry herself, but is that concept applied to or expected from the men who date female pastors? Do we not need the same level of care and support in our ministries as our male counterparts?

Dating someone who doesn't want to be a part of my life as a pastor never goes well. It becomes a juggling act for me as I try to make time to nurture that relationship and fulfill my ministerial commitments. Trying to be a church and community leader means being active in those things, and if my partner isn't with me, then we aren't spending much time together, and the relationship suffers and ultimately ends. Then what? Do I start the process over again, or should I spread it out a bit? If I decide to install that dating app again, should I match with several and go out on dates with them all at once? These might seem like silly questions, but really, do the same rules apply to me as a pastor as they do to other women? Think about it, are women that actively date or talk to several men seen in a positive light? You would think that people would want me to date different people to ensure I find the best one for me. I think it goes back to the mentality that if I'm dating, I must be ready to remarry, that getting married must be the goal of my dating instead of dating for dating's sake. Dating, for me, has to begin with friendship and progress into something more based on common values and our ability to vibe with one another. And that takes time and isn't necessarily done one at a time. It's possible to talk to and get to know several people at once, and it's the ideal way to date if you truly want to find the right person. What I have found interesting is that my male colleagues don't seem to be burdened with the same scrutiny and judgment while dating.

The Warning:

After my separation and divorce and during my discernment and call into the Ministry, one of my mentors, realizing that I would soon be a single female pastor, shared a true story with me that I still carry with me today. He told me that a newly ordained minister was called as the associate pastor in a church in his community. This new pastor was a young, single, attractive man and, because of that, had been receiving some attention from various women in the church. One of his congregants contacted him very upset and concerned about something that she was going through. She told him she was in need of pastoral care and asked if he would please come to her home. The associate pastor had met with this congregant and her husband before and knew that they were having marital issues. He was concerned about her and decided to make a home visit to try to console her, but when he arrived, he found her dressed very provocatively, and he realized that her husband was not home. It became apparent to him quite quickly that he was not there to provide pastoral care and that she intended to seduce him. Unfortunately, he gave in to his desires and had an affair with the woman. Somehow people found out about the affair, and subsequently, his ministry was ruined, he was fired from his position at the church, and he lost his standing as clergy. I think my mentor chose to tell me this story for two reasons. To help me understand that indiscretions like that of the young pastor can lead to huge repercussions and that, as a newly single woman being called into ministry, I need to be guarded about people's intentions. I've come to realize that there are people who place pastors on a pedestal, they view them as being holy or superhuman, and they enjoy trying to bend or break their boundaries to see if the pastor can be tempted. To see if they will cross the line. Thankfully, I haven't experienced anyone like this in my parish ministry, but my online ministry platform is rampant with people trying to tempt me with all kinds of things.

Unwanted Online Attention And Its Effect On My Ministry:

I joined the many ministers in 2020 who began to live stream my services so I could continue my ministry during the pandemic. It's truly been a blessing to my ministry in many ways, but in my personal life, not so much. I began using my personal social media account to share my weekly message and reach more people. When people send me a friend request, I always accept them in the hope that my ministry might extend to another person. Sometimes these new friends send private messages asking for an opportunity to sit down and chat. Given that it's part of my ministry, I say yes and excitedly meet the person in a public arena to have a conversation. Unfortunately, there have been times that I've met someone thinking that it was an extension of my ministry or pastoral care, only to find out that, in their eyes, it was a date. I've had men who watch my online service come into the sanctuary on Sunday and seemingly become part of the church, only to find out that it was in the hope that they might be able to build a personal relationship with me. I've concluded that it's less about me and more about the idea of dating a woman in ministry that appeals to them. What they don't know is that pastors have a ministerial code of

ALL THE PREACHER'S WIVES
A Peek Behind The Curtain Of Being A Preacher's Wife

ethics, and there are certain boundaries that we do have to draw. Those boundaries give us the ability to minister and provide pastoral care to those in our congregation. It isn't easy to figure out how to navigate that line between when a boundary needs to be set and when it's crucial to provide that pastoral presence to someone in a moment in which they need it. I find myself on constant guard in various situations as I'm trying to figure out exactly what's taking place and discern the intentions of those who contact me. It's hard not to be skeptical. At one point, my frustrations with heightened unwanted attention from males watching my service online led me to mention it to my church secretary, who suggested I start wearing an engagement ring during the live stream. I have to admit I considered it but decided I didn't want engagement rumors to start circulating, which would create a whole other issue I'd need to address. When men use my church or ministry to try to build a personal relationship with me, it creates a problem as I try to navigate that situation, so I don't discourage them from coming to church but try to deter them from asking me on dates.

Then there are the guys that just don't have a clue. They slide into my DM's with something like, "If you were my pastor, I'd be at church every Sunday." I honestly don't know how to respond appropriately to statements like that, so I just don't respond at all. On a few not-so-pleasant occasions in which, I received private messages or DM's that escalated to the point of being asked out or being shown attention that I didn't want to reciprocate, in my kindest, most polite way, try to refocus the person back towards their interest in my ministry and not in a relationship. I was accused of not being a very good person or pastor because I didn't receive their advances to go on a date in the way that they hoped.

When thinking about dating someone in general, I am cautious. Some of these men have social media accounts that are full of things that I wouldn't want to be associated with, like over-sexualized and offensive posts and derogatory remarks. I'm a pastor, yes, but my willingness to be open and accepting for the sake of the Gospel doesn't carry into my dating life. I will minister to and share the

Gospel with anyone, but that has nothing to do with wanting them to be a part of my personal life. I'm very guarded in my social media interactions to the point that if I receive a private message or a DM from someone and they begin talking about my ministry or my church, I've started letting them know that because of their interest in my ministry, I am ethically bound to view them as members of my congregation. That way, if their interest seems to become more about a personal relationship than my ministry, I can let them know dating congregants is prohibited.

What I've Concluded:

There's an assumption that if a pastor is single, they must be actively looking for a life partner; because pastors are expected to be married and participate in ministry together. What most people don't consider is that many pastors meet their significant others either while attending college or seminary or in the early stages of their life before they are ordained and called to be the pastor of a church. So that relationship naturally grows and functions as that couple support one another through that call into ministry. Often the person dating the future pastor beings to be an active part of their ministry, but what if the pastor's life doesn't follow that norm? Like in my case? I never considered how difficult it would be as a divorced mother with two sons, sharing a home with my mother, to successfully date. I once had a female colleague tell me, "You're not two people; you're always "just" Jamie (that encompasses my family life, my aspirations, and dreams, and all the parts of me that make up "me") and Pastor Jamie (that's whom God has created and called me to be in this world through ministry and service)," but in my dating experience, that's not been true. Maybe that's why I'm still single. What I have noticed is that the men who reach out to me after watching a worship service want to date Pastor Jamie, and the men I meet through chance encounters and online dating platforms, want to date "just" Jamie. To date successfully, the person I date would have to be all in. They'd have to be able to be a part of my life and my ministry. It's hard enough trying to find someone willing to be faithfully committed in a relationship, much less extending that faithful commitment and support to their partner's ministry. Wish me luck; a few prayers wouldn't hurt, either.

ABOUT THE AUTHORS

The authors of this anthology are each celebrated for their courage and honesty. The fact is there were others who were approached for this anthology that may have been uncomfortable or unable to speak as freely as the 20 wonderful women of this book at the time. Collectively and individually, the women of *All The Preacher's Wives* hope that their words bring encouragement and hope to you.

For those women contributors who are currently married to men in ministry, understand that each discussed this project with their husbands respectively. Accordingly, each husband endorsed and embraced this opportunity for their wives to share their truth. This book is not independently written by those women but with the loving support of their husbands.

The thought of this book came to Author N. D. "Indy" Brennan during a conversation with fellow author and anthology contributor Melanie M. Johnson. At the time, neither realized the effect this book would have on the world. It was Coach Krystal Henry during a subsequent conversation who first mentioned the anthology was much more than a book. It was the birth of a ministry and sisterhood. Since these earlier conversations, each contributor of the book has expressed similar sentiments. Thank you for allowing God to use you and to initiate a sisterhood that shall have a lifelong positive and spiritual uplifting effect.

Please visit www.allthepreacherswives.com for bookings and to learn more about the women of this anthology.

ALL THE PREACHER'S WIVES
A Peek Behind The Curtain Of Being A Preacher's Wife

www.ingramcontent.com/pod-product-compliance
Lightning Source LLC
Chambersburg PA
CBHW042028050526
44107CB00103B/733